Through It All,
JESUS
Kept Me Strong!

Elisheva

abbott press®

A DIVISION OF WRITER'S DIGEST

Abbott Press books may be ordered through booksellers or by contacting:

Abbott Press
1663 Liberty Drive
Bloomington, IN 47403
www.abbottpress.com
Phone: 1-866-697-5310

ISBN: 978-1-4582-1020-3 (sc)
ISBN: 978-1-4582-1019-7 (e)

Library of Congress Control Number: 2013911310

Printed in the United States of America.

Abbott Press rev. date: 6/24/2013

Table of Contents

Intro song: I'll tell the Story and you'll turn the page. 'll tell the story and you'll turn the page, i'll tell the story and you'll turn the page, I'll tell the story and you'll turn the page. Young girl young girl you don't have to be afraid....the decisions of your life you made, girl it's gonna be okay, Jesus is your rock and your salvation! If you'll only take his hand you'll see you have a second chance listen to my testimony and I pray this will encourage you...Turn the page, I'll tell the story and you'll turn the page, I'll tell the story and you'll turn the page, I'll tell the story and you'll Turn the page, I'll tell the story and you'll you just turn the page....This is the story of a young girl and how her life was changed, she was the victim of a cruel world she didn't know the game, born into this life she's looking for love anywhere looking to her mother and father but they never seemed to be care, where did I go from here? Who can I trust to be there in my life, God told me that everything would be okay, So why is my life in so much pain.... so much pain....turn the page. (written by: Elisheva !!)

Song #1 We Need Love: (written by: Elisheva!!)

I think we need love baby, I think we need love baby, I think we need love... I think we need love baby yeah...I think we need love baby, I think we need love. Hook.

Verse: I think we need love baby, to spread out to our girls young lady.... cause they don't have a clue, that we're like diamonds and pearls ladies, don let it get you down lady God will turn it right around lady, He's got ya back so smile and girl remember who you are!

Hook: God knows we need love baby, God think we need love baby, God knows we need love...God think we need love baby yeah, God knows we need love baby.

Verse #2: Just a little faith baby and things are gonna change lady, this one thing is true troubles they don last always ohhh nooo, No matter what they say baby God will bring a change lady, He will make your dreams come true remember God believes in you !

Hook: I know we need love baby, I think we need love baby, I think we need love…I know we need love baby yeaaa, I think we need love baby, I think we need love!

Bridge: Tears falling from your eyes, let God will wipe them dry baby and hold on, sister you can carry on. If you can dream it, you will see it! Just believe it sister you'll achieve it oh oh love, love, love!

Hook: I know we need love baby, I think we need love, I think we need love…I know we need love baby yea! I think we need love baby, Through Jesus there's love!

Song #2 Dream, Wait: (Written by: Elisheva & LR!!)

Verse 1: dream wait, wait and dream wishing for you to love me. A hurtful past I'm crawling fast to your arms, but you don't know. I would cry and shed these tears throughout the years, Love love, your the one to set me free, please set me free. I dream a dream…

Hook: I wanna wait for you boy, I wanna wait here for you boy, nobody else can hold my heart,. No body else could hold my heart. I wanna wait for you boy, wanna wait here for you boy. Nobody else can hold my heart…la da da dad a!

Verse 2: Love hate, I'm hating love... cause boy with you I just don't know I tried to pack my things and go. But I'm still chained up in my soul! I still cry and shed the tears throughout the years, love, love. Your the one, you set me free, you set me free, I dream I dream...

Hook; I wanna wait for you love, I wanna wait here for you love. Nobody else can hold my heart, Nobody else can hold my heart. I wanna wait for you love! I wanna wait here for you love, nobody else can hold my heart!

Bridge: I wanna be there in your arms, I should have saw this from the start, when we I first stared into your eyes, I felt your passion inside me (high!) I need your love please stay with me! Don't keep me dreaming, come to me please set me free!

Ending; Don't keep me dreaming, come back to me. Come back come back come back.

Interlude: The Streets Are Oh They Talking! (Written By: Latoya and Reese!!)

the streets are oh they talking, the streets are cold so watch It! On the streets I know I can make it anywhere I go. Any any where I go, any anywhere I go, any anywhere I go! any anywhere I go!

Hey ladies you know about them cuties? Always talking about some booty, Just because we went to dinner and movie I'm not on you not at all. Wrong girl and the wrong song! you can miss me with that and just take me home! wrong girl and the wrong song you can miss me with that and just take me home!

Song #3: Make It Count!! (Written by Elisheva!!) !!

Hook!: Yea, yea, yea, yea yes Lord! Love is calm, Give me the power! make it count, make it count, Imma imma, imma, imma make it count! Make it count Lord make It count, Imma, imma, imma, imma, imma, make it count!

Verse:

Jesus is the Word and the Word is God, His spirit is in my soul! For everything you did you gave your Son for me this sacrifice is incredible! Your grace and your mercy set me free, for this I belong to you! Please use me Lord for what you need me for! I'll do it all for you! Give it all for you!

Hook: Make it count imma, imma, imma make it count! Make it count Lord make it count Imma, Imma, Imma, Imma, Imma make it count!

Bridge: Oh Lord, You are the love of my life! I've never known a love like this before! Everyone else don't understand. You've been my lover, you've been my friend, you've been my healer, you've been my lawyer, you've been right there for me! I'll never let you gooo! I feel you in my soul! Your Love is like FIRE to my bones!!! And Imma make it count for you! You made my dreams come true when I found out that your spirit lives within me LORD IT'S YOU!!! Make it count imma, imma, imma, imma, imma, make it count! Make it count Lord make it count Imma imma imma, imma, make it count!

Ending! I need you I love you it's soo true your amazing to me! I need you, I love you, I praise you everyday! Sunlight you bring to me you breathe the life in me! I wanna make it count for you!!!

Chapter One

I WAS BORN NOV, 2, 1980 at 12:08 pm at St. Elizabeth hospital. Born to Ayelle Roberts age 19 and a father who was never there Johnathan Edwards age 21. It was not but soon after my mother's father had died I guess my mom was looking for love. Unfortunately she got a kid out of it and a neglectful child's father. Johnathan ended up marrying his high school sweetheart and just left my mother and me out to the world.

What do I mean by this you may be asking? "Laughing" Let's just say as we go a little further into my life story you'll understand what I mean. We often look to the world for love or our own needs instead of GOD. He is the only one to deliver us!! Often times we as people seek to find love in others, and forget that GOD our Living Father is the only true love we have if only we would put him first and worship him as well as keeping his LAWS and COMMANDMENTS! But we go astray and I know better than anyone how being blinded by ignorance and not knowing Yahweh truly, you began to get led astray.

You seek this love in people. The Devil uses this as a tool to prevent you from realizing GOD's love for you. As you continue to read you will understand just what I mean as the events of my life unfold. In the beginning of my journey before I was even born, my mother went to get an abortion.

My mother told me that she was sitting there debating on going through with the process of an abortion and she said I don't really want to get an abortion. She sat there remembering the commandment of the LORD THY GOD, Thou shalt not kill!

It was at that moment she had decided to back out of getting an abortion after all. When her time had come up, the receptionist had called her name. She went in and the nurse asked her if she was ready? My mother then stated at that moment I have decided on keeping my child. The nurse then said to my mother (You don't want to do this). Certainly if you make this choice you will be ruining your future but my mother said, I am going to keep my baby. This nurse was so persistent in trying to get my mother to get rid of me. That's when my mother had to practically yell at this woman to get her to understand. Well my mother walked out with her child still growing in her womb!

After having me my mom had not her own place and had to go live at home with my grandmother Mrs. Lori Joelyn. This was very hard for her being that she had a responsibility to raise a child now and decided to sign up for welfare. What a drag.... but it did come in handy for a young woman and her child. I asked my mom what happened once my dad knew I was home from the hospital, and that he had a baby girl in the world to take care of? Her response was that he held me and didn't look too pleased at my looks. As if I was not good enough.

My dad looked me head to toe. I was a high yellow almost white complicated baby that he didn't think would be to appealing to the human eye…lol, but in my mom's words. UGLY. Mom always did tell it like it is. I guess that was the true beginning of why my self- esteem was low? It began from the feeling of my dad does not want me because of how I look. So I began to feel as if no one would love me and that I always had to be accepted as a child.

When mom asked him if he was going to help her take care of me his response was "all I have is five dollars." Now of coarse when I was little I had enough sense already to know that when my mom would purchase things for me five dollars was not going to cover a darn thing! I just looked at my mommy and placed my head on her shoulder and arms around her and she embraced me. But still I blamed her for my dad's absence. My mother had told me that she would never beg him for a dime after the way he had treated her and I! I was so wrong to do so but too young to understand.

I had no idea of what was really going on or why. When you are a child you have so many questions. We who are parents now know this all too well for our children drown us in questions all of the time so I know you can relate to this. I try to remember as much as I can about my childhood. Not much comes up that's good, but only a few memories. Most were pretty bad times it wasn't until I became an adult did I realize how hard it was for her. I had to learn this lesson once I became a mother but we'll get to that later once again.

So where did my daddy go your wondering? Well you guys that's a question I've asked myself for many years and guess what? He left and went back home. Crazy thing is he didn't leave the state, he didn't go to the military, or prison…Yup you got it he sat right in the same town living his life with his wife who never bore any children. Chose her over my whole existence. He got with his high school sweetheart and he just wouldn't claim me. One thing some men don't get is when you leave the mother you leave the child and some mothers don't always make the best decision that's why it's so important that you at least be man enough to show up in your children's lives!

Don't be mistaken this is book is not to bash my mother nor struggling mothers such as myself who have made a lot of bad choices. It is to explain my mistakes and life experiences and that GOD is the only way. If only we would realize these things before hand and listen to GOD. Sometimes we as human beings don't understand that we put ourselves through more than we have to. Yahweh does not mean for us to struggle and sometimes even when we do it brings us closer to him with a humbled heart! If you would read the book of Hosea, you will see that GOD even says himself that his children suffer due to lack of understanding.

Often times we lean unto our own understandings in life instead of his commandments for us to live righteously! Something I myself know all too well. I think I have violated every rule that GOD has ever spoken. The greatest joy I get is that our Father sent JESUS here to save us from our sins and Jesus himself prepares a place in heaven for all who come to him by confessing him as our LORD and SAVIOR as well as repenting for our sins!

In Matthew chapter 4 verse 4 Jesus himself said, "It is written: 'Man shall not live by bread alone, but by every word that comes from out of the mouth of GOD. The question is do we listen? GOD loves us so much but yet we all seek after our own heart's desire. Some of which in my very case don't even know what we want, where we're going, or what GOD wanted for our lives. Drowned in our own fantasies of success. Some of us get it, and others just chase the dream by imagining all day long trying to run away from our reality. Not knowing that our lives are more than just physical but way more spiritual than you have ever known if we just ask GOD.

So we stayed with my grandmother in which everything was not peaches and cream. See my grandmother was from good ole shy town. South side of Chicago and she was young and met Leon Jr. who was from Ohio and she fell in love with him and got married, had children, you know how it goes. My family was hardworking and had a strong love for each other.

They had seven children.... NIcole, Ayelle my mom, Leon, Andrea who passed away as an infant, Rochelle, my beloved aunt who's no longer with us, Jayone, and Ella. Surprisingly they were a lot closer once! Boy if you would have known just how much. This at least makes me smile. My grandfather worked for the steel mill before they closed them all down and all the money left the town of Youngstown, Ohio.

This affected many families. But sadly my grandfather was shot and killed. It was said that he was shot in his back by his best friend. Human kind always had a murderous spirit since the beginning of time. In the beginning just as you will still find to this day in the book of Genesis, how Cain killed his own brother in chapter 4 verse 8. I am reading out of the NIV bible but I'm certain you can find this story in yours along with the fall of man. So the family was family but much more separated.

I sometimes wonder where everyone would be had not this had happened?

Chapter Two

Black Sheep

I WAS ALWAYS TOLD WE were often kicked out of grandma's house in which led her to meet a man who in the beginning seemed very nice but looks of coarse are deceiving. See the story is said that upon my grandfather's death there was big money involved in which was left to my mom.

My mom being young couldn't understand and was given papers to sign by my grandmother. She asked what they were about and my grandmother just said sign them they are about your daddy for a tombstone. My mom did not read those papers or anything but because this was her mother she did as she was told. I used to often wonder why my mother was treated as the black sheep of the family or why she was always being beaten up on? Funny thing is the family including my grandmother said that the money never existed and that my mother was just crazy. Funny thing is now for some reason after all these years my mother is receiving mail to this day with my grandfather's social security number attached to hers on her most recent statements. Seeing this made me cry at

32 years old because, I once sided with my family over her calling her crazy and saying that none of it was true.

I guess I see now just how hurtful family can be after all these years all of the truth is being revealed even things I didn't know were. I thank GOD for his words and for Jesus being my LORD and SAVIOR. GOD had already spoken about jealousy long before any of our existence. Perfect example, the crucifixion of JESUS CHRIST!

The Scribes and Pharisees rejected our savior. No, I AM NOT COMPARING MYSELF TO JESUS... EVER! I am simply trying to show you something I lacked in knowledge myself not too long ago. Stories of our Savior, and how cruel people can be. That's one of the reasons I am so thankful. Everything that anyone has ever went through in life is in the Holy Bible. My family fought each other so often physically that the Youngstown Police Department knew my family by name. I know my mom has major attitude problems and boy does she have a way with words but this was deeper than that I just had no idea until now.

My mom had finally gotten her own place but there was no gas on in the house and it was very cold so my mom would bundle me up as much as she could in a bunch of clothes from the trash bags they were filled in. She said that one day a man just walked in the house and said I've been watching you and she was afraid. But he then told her not to be scared and asked "you need help don't you"? She told me she cried because she knew she did and he was not the most attractive site but she did need help because we barely had any food. So when offered she took it. She said she couldn't be more thankful because she didn't have anyone else.

I must say even though we struggled extremely hard, everything happens for a reason. This man fed us, helped clothe me, and helped to provide shelter. At the ages from 1 to 3 he was the only dad I had ever known. Until one day I asked the question that every mother who has this secret dreads. Mom is he really my dad? Because I started noticing the arguments, when he would say she ain't my daughter any ways. So my mom eventually had that confession. Soon later he became a father to my brother Keon Jr. I was about four years old then and very happy to know I was going to be a big sister!

Only problem was I often wondered why this man would beat my mother repeatedly. My brother was born and he was the most beautiful thing I had ever seen in my little life. I was truly amazed! He was always getting into something though lol. He used to pop me in the head with his bottle. Believe it or not he was very strong! We had one of those little color televisions. You know the ones where when your floor model television would go out and stop working, so your parents went and got the little color television and set it on top of the big one lol. Well my little one year old brother somehow picked this little one up when it was sitting on the floor and carried it. He was a funny, cute, chubby, little one to me. This memory makes me smile because we don't have many of them, we were pretty much divided. Two years later I was a big sister again! My mom had another little girl and named her Salene. She too was gorgeous! I loved her so much and still do. But we too are divided.

Big Keon kept on and kept on abusing my mom and would use the kids to prevent her from leaving. He was an addict and a drinker and she drank as well. Crack cocaine and heroine was the big thing in the era of the 80's. She would try to leave with her children but she couldn't get away, and one day it went just too far. She left and took me with her. Keon would not let her get my brother and sister and leave. Believe me he was not the best candidate for the job of keeping my brother and sister, dad or not! You will learn why. My mom had a lot of boyfriends back then and often they were abusive. It would always be little old me trying to fight to get a man off of her.

I remember this one guy named Smith who had a lot of money and all this gold jewelry on all of the time. He bought my mom a real fur coat! My mom was very beautiful and skinny with a walk to die for! Boy she was so proud of that coat.

I don't have that walk though lol. I remember him beating on my mother and never seeing him again after that.

Chapter Three

Molestation and Rape

THEN ANOTHER GUY NAMED RICK. Then we were alone again most of times but my mom would drop me off at a cousins house and always come back with money. But this cousin was not a person to leave your child around. Just put it this way they teach you in school that there are certain places children should not be touched by adults in nasty ways. My first but faint encounter of molestation was when my mom had left me in the projects with my cousins while she went out for a while. I remember the heavier of the twin brothers who were our cousins telling me to lay down in this room and all of the lights were off. I was scared and nervous at the same time. He pulled down my panties and his hands were touching me in my private areas. When I told my mom, of course she flipped. But I remember a lot of yelling, someone always touching your damn daughter. Thing is a lot of other children were being abused too but it was always being hushed? That's right yall I was always being violated by a relative in the family, this is very true but no one wanted to tell the truth. And for telling the truth, we were always being thrown out or I had to constantly watch my mom fight or get jumped.

Before this I was also told that I was raped by my uncle as well. Story goes that at the age of 2 my mother had left out for a while. Leaving me with my then younger aunt and uncle Jayone and Ella. They had fallen asleep in the next room and my eldest uncle Leon the 3rd had just gotten out of a half way home for the rape of a young girl. I had on a blue dress with little white and blue laced ruffles.

My mother said she came home and I was sitting in a chair in the corner on the left side of the room. She picked me up and my legs were stiff. She kept trying to get me to respond but I had this shocked blank look on my face. She tried to pry my legs open but I would not bend. So she took me in my grandmother's room and laid me down on her bed. She looked at my face, and my chest and arms.

Still she said she noticed nothing out of the ordinary. So my mother began to run me a warm bath. Took off my clothes, tested the water, and put me in the tub. I began to scream and my mother snatched me out, ran me back into my grandmother's room, and had laid me on the bed screaming what's the matter? What's wrong baby? She tried to open my legs but I still would not budge so she had to force them apart and then she saw.... all of my skin on my little vagina cut all over my vaginal.

Now I remember many of things but I asked GOD why I couldn't remember this tragic event? When I asked this question again at the age I am now of 32 GOD spoke using my mentor as the vessel and said he would not allow this memory for as a child I was not able to bear and understand such things. So I count this event as a blessing because it shows of how much GOD loves me even

11

though I had to bear such things. GOD still gets all the glory! For everything I have been through there is no way GOD does not exist!! Jehovah Jireh is very real and he has great patience with us now more than ever before, especially since GOD gave his only Son JESUS CHRIST!

I cry even now. My oldest aunt said that my mother was a liar along with my great aunts, grandmother and many more. JESUS says for us to love our enemies in Luke chapter 6 verses 27-37. For vengeance is mine thus saith the LORD thy GOD! Woe now unto those who go on thinking that what they do in darkness is covered for GOD the creator of all life does see all, and nothing is hidden! I shall not be the judge of any wrong done unto me but I tell you GOD has not forgotten. If these things had not taken place I would not have a story to tell and not be able to share with you just how much GOD loves us all and is with us through all of our trials and tribulations. He will never leave us nor forsake us but it is us who leave GOD.

This sickens me to my stomach that grown adult men will even think of a child in a sexual manner but the devil attacks the mind, body, and spirit. Just as the LORD our GOD has his vessels so does the adversary. I have forgiven all finally, but the cost I had to pay for telling what happened to me was no picnic either. I had to always be taken into the emergency room at St. Elizabeth hospital for these types of issues and I guess finally my mom got tired and called children services. My mother had given me to the system this last time when one of my eldest cousins had molested me. Yes my mom would come and visit me and I loved seeing her. Just before that she took me to the hospital I was actually admitted and I was watching JESUS of Nazareth for the first time. I was six years old at the time when then one of my oldest cousin Drake had touched me in forbidden places and that's when I made my first best friend. It was after my mom left from seeing me that I was watching this movie and I saw how they nailed Jesus to the cross after all his beauty and miracles. I was terribly hurt and I cried so hard and started praying. Now back then St. Elizabeth still had nuns working there and this one nun came in to check on me only to see me crying. She was very beautiful to me and sweet. I cannot remember her name but I call her my first best friend because she explained what and why this happened to JESUS while I was watching this. And I still love her dearly for this wherever she may be. My GOD bless her.

She said to me oh you sweet child you understand a little about what they have done and I said yes ma'am and she hugged me and said GOD loves me and that's why JESUS had died because he loved us so much and she told me it's going to be okay and to go to bed.

I was glad to have her there I felt safe. From that day on during my stay there in the hospital she would always bring me orange popsicles and gram crackers and soda! I loved her. This woman would come and play with puzzle games with me and color in the place where the play room used to be for kids. But one day I did not see her again and I remember getting out of the bed and searching for her only to come to a room with other nuns and they said she was not there.

I never saw her again and this made me very upset. I think of her often still to this day and wish I knew her name. I thank GOD for her because she was sweet and peaceful kids need that. Even then at that age I knew not that the LORD will send his people in times of trouble to bring forth comfort in his name. I wonder if she may have been an angel? To show forth that GOD lives and is the creator of all. This wouldn't be the last time GOD would send beautiful experiences in my life.

See what I didn't know until now is that we often just reference GOD in the ages of old or what we go to the churches and hear. GOD still lives. He is the living GOD and still hears his people and prayers just the same as the generations of old. GOD never changes we change and do not understand the things in which we do in our journeys of life. It is us who do not listen to him. Still searching for love, money, power...... I have found that I have not truly discovered life until I discovered GOD who is the creator of all things and the living GOD!!

I am still learning.

Chapter Four

Foster Care and back again....

NOW I DON'T KNOW RATHER it was that particular hospital stay or one last visit because every time I looked up I was there...but some woman by the name of Annie came into the room and my mom was there and my mom had explained to me I was gonna have to leave for a while. I didn't understand, because I wanted to go home with my mom! How come my mother couldn't go where I was going?

This woman said I was going to be safe and go to a new place until my mom and I are able to be together again. When I think about that day this memory still causes some pain of unhealed wounds.

She said there would be other kids there and no one would bother me again. So we had that whole heartbreaking moment where the child aka me was crying, kicking, and screaming for my mom while my mom was just standing there in tears upset and ready to go crazy but she had to be calm.

They took me. I was in and out of many different homes and can't remember them all. The first person to ever have custody was my cousin who was supposed to be my god mother. I don't like this term of expression anyways. She actually had helped to name me when I was born. Well she had become blinded by life and love in which there was abuse in her own life. I remember her punching me in my nose a few times especially when my cousin and I had homework and my biggest academic issue was math. It got to a point where I feared math and refused to learn it due to this.

Fear of being mocked every time I got a question wrong so I just let that one go at an early age. I remember her stealing the donation money I collected for UNICEF, I had no idea about drug addiction. All I knew was, in school they taught us to say no to drugs back in the 80's. So eventually I was taken from there. There was only one nice woman with a nice clean house and she would dress me and this other little girl up so very pretty with ruffle dresses, I actually slept without having to watch out for any creeps.

Then I was moved again. House to house. Some had guys who would make me stand over them with my legs spread in a darn dress. A little freaking girl, "are you serious"? You must be joking to take me from one screwed up situation to another. So I remained visiting my mom while they would watch me through a dark black glass window and always had to depart from her in the end. The dark black glass I used to think. Where you watch what you say because you're being monitored. You barely get to be comfortable with your own child because you feel like a prisoner.

Trying to explain why you get to have these meetings that they call visits with your own baby! I couldn't stand it. Each time I felt as if my heart was being ripped right out of me, and I was alone…just alone. I wonder about the system? Even now they still take a child from a situation but some still end up coming out of it abused, hooked on drugs, beaten and raped, even murdered. Final house lower south side, one old woman and her grandsons she was taking care of due to her daughter's passing in which I felt sad for them about. That had to be hard. I couldn't understand them either.

They used to call me ugly, beat me up, try being sexual with me, tell lies to get me in trouble if I didn't do what they say, and lock me in the closet with bags over my head and wouldn't let me out when she was gone. I hated that house. I mean I truly did. What do children even know about sex? Let's just say the corruption of children in this world goes on and on but GOD will put an end to it all!

One day I stole a colored picture to give my mom so she could think I made it for her. The 8th commandment! This woman found out and beat the dog mess out of me, I mean if you could have seen the whelp marks from the big thick leather belt you would have wanted to hurt her yourself. All and all stealing is wrong. Funny thing I didn't understand is why she would have been goofy enough to put me on an short outfit with short sleeves knowing I had a visit to see my mom at children services, and boy my mother flipped I mean she was ready to fight this woman and these people over her child!

This truly upset her. So my mom threatened to sue them if they had not had me home by my eighth birthday. Which she was absolutely right to because she had done her part by getting a stable home, enrolled at Youngstown State University, and gotten married to a cab driver Mr. Wilis Baskott. So why not give her back her child?

And so they did. On my eighth birthday I had come home to meet my family that I had no memory of. In only that little bit of time I was barely able to remember anyone but my mother. After my party and meeting my cousin's I was enrolled in school. I had my best holidays at home that first year! My mom was working, home was cozy, and for once I felt here I belonged, but this too ended very soon.

There was unfaithfulness in my mom's marriage in which had broken the bond between man and wife. I began to see that in some families scandal was just swept under the rug and we were to just keep it hush hush…but if an eight year old little girl knew that this life was wrong and you were to be righteous and honest to one another how come the adults that raised us were not believers in this righteousness?

I saw firsthand how wicked towards one another people can be. But we will come back to this shortly. One day my aunt Rochelle had called and I guess she was having a party for her kids and she asked my mom if I could come over? Well due to the way the family was and things of that nature my mom said no. But me as a child just excited to go and play with my cousins I kept begging to go and I wanted to be accepted, I still never felt accepted by my family because I was very different from beginning. So I begged and my mom said yes finally. So she and my step dad finally allowed me to go.

Chapter Five

MY AUNT ROCHELLE CAME AND got me and we did have fun my cousin's and I. I had fun playing and laughing. It got late and I remember my cousins laying in the room with my aunt. I ended up sleeping downstairs my where my other aunt Ella was. I remember hearing a knock at the door, my aunt Ella yelled who is it? It was my other known pedifile cousin and she refused to let him into the house. I went back to sleep and while asleep after a good while, I kept feeling weird touches in my vaginal area. And feeling strange.

I woke up and saw the brother of the jerk in the family who touches children, his name was Ray. He was the oldest brother of Drake who touched me before, I hated them as a child. If I could not remember many family it was for darn sure I could never forget those two pedifiles!! I lifted up the covers and saw that my pants and panties were pulled down to my ankles and at that moment he whispered to me "Don't scream..., Shhh"!

Drake and Ray were not the kind of guys you could leave your children with. It's a shame that grown men would do such things to children.

I looked at him and I got up and put this sheet around my body and proceeded up the stairs into the bathroom. I looked down there and noticed my body was very wet down there in my little area where I was taught NO ONE was supposed to touch! I then wiped myself off and pulled up my panties. Not knowing that when violated you don wipe anything but I was still just a little girl.

I began to cry and scream so loud it woke up my aunt Rochelle and her kids! She was like "what's the matter?" I was crying and screaming and ran to her and I told her that he had touched me in my vagina and I pointed at him...She grabbed me and said.... Hell No!!! He begged her not to say anything and soon switched his story in front of the both of us and tried calling me a little liar.

After that all I remember is my mom very pissed off. I don't remember how my cousin actually ended up in prison serving a life sentence. But he is. It was said that murder is one reason and I guess also because of his obsession with fondling little children. I don't really know.

My mom had come and got me once my aunt Rochelle called. They ended up fighting pretty bad and my mom took me and left. When I got home I was bathed and clothed into my p.j.s and then she had given me my teddy bear and my blanket. Then the questions began about what happened?

The police were involved but they said that because my mom was not there she could not make a statement. So we went no further I just stayed home. One day we were over to my grandmother's house and we saw this child pervert there as well. My family was planning a trip to Cedar Point and all the kids were going except for me so of course I wanted to go. I asked if I could go but my mom and step dad said NO!! Because of what had happened to me and this cousin was still coming around after he did what he did with no one saying a thing because they were used to covering up family scandals and the fact that I would always tell pissed them off.

See the time when my uncle raped me was covered and hushed as well. See he never got jail time. It was said that the family some of which who are great aunt's had money, ties with mafia, masons, and knew some big people. Back then my mother was said to be the loony by the family. This was also because there were rumors about money she was supposed to receive back when her father died that she never got. It went missing mysteriously and everyone knew nothing of it. I always thought she was nuts myself but just this past Christmas my mom got a letter in the mail with my grandfather's social security number attached to hers ? But we are wondering why because they all denied it and we never received anything. If all these years her mother, brothers and sisters stated that it never existed she's crazy, then why is this letter surfacing after all these years, and why come she was always denied when she would go to social security to find out? Truth but a lot of unanswered questions. That's just the way things went and I didn't understand it.

The whole thing was just crooked, but back to the issue of the sexual predators in the family. So over hearing my mom and step dad's conversation the pedifile cousin and one of the so called uncles decided to physically jump on my step dad because of what he said in the defense of his family! It was horrible come to think about it they were always jumping on my mom! I never did go to Cedar Point. It's funny because when I became an adult I remember this pedifile calling over to my grandmother's house. Once he had discovered I was there he asked to speak to me.

I didn't want to get the phone but he begged to speak to me. Grabbing the phone in anger I said hello...and he had asked me to forgive him. I asked him why he did what he did and he couldn't explain it. I told him I forgive him but could never understand for the life of me what would make a grown man touch a child sexually? Still to this day I don't have the answer.

Unfortunately my mom's marriage ended up failing because of unfaithfulness and more lies and scandal. My step dad ended up cheating with some woman just a few blocks away from my mom and get this his sneaky behind even ended up hanging round with my mom's sisters I'll say no more. Just put it this way there shall never be a time when you can't trust your family around your spouse but in this family honey...WATCH YOUR MARRIAGE!

I too fell victim to some of my family curses. Sleeping with a relative child's dad in my past. Guilty of past scandal, I was no innocent Sally once I had become an adult. Even as a teenager I was not listening to GOD!

Chapter Six

THEY DIVORCED AND WE LOST our house, car and the little money we had. Mom never returned to YSU and began drinking more and more with her family. What we had was not much but it was what GOD blessed us to have and sometimes you don't know what blessings you truly have until you've lost them. So my mom went back to what she knew. That's what we do make up with one another and sweep it away until you get drunk enough to remember the hurt again forget about the forgiveness and then the fighting starts again.

We moved into the house with my grandmother on the east side of town. The best fun was with my cousins running around and playing. I'll never forget when we all got in trouble for smoking cigarettes even though Edwardo my little cousin was the one who got caught with it lol. I was ten years old and only the joy of playing with my cousins made me feel like I was actually accepted.

Taysahwna, Edwardo, and Consuella! But I often wanted to play and grow up with my own brother and sister. I began to wonder GOD why come my life is so rough? When will this sadness end? Why come my family members look at me so strange and at times don't want to look at me when I smile at all? Often they roll their eyes? All these questions…but no answers! GOD was always quiet.

At least that's what I used to think as a little girl. I remember one evening my mom came in very drunk and was going change into some different clothes I don't know how it started I just remember a bunch of yelling and my uncle telling my mom to get the f#%k out her and her lying little b#%&h of a daughter!

Somebody always raping your daughter or touching on just her just get the f#%k out! My mom had ended up putting on that fur coat from years before and had my hand and we left. She was getting ready to try and take a bath during all this. He put her out without anything on but that coat and she was too drunk to realize it. Honestly I think she was high off of something more than liquor that night. My mom and I walked around all night and she was pissy drunk while I kept clinging to her hand all night just praying that nothing would happen to us.

I just looked up to the sky at night and said God please I don't know what to do? She didn't have on anything but that dang fur coat. How could he?

My mom was slowly getting sober as the light was also slowly coming through the clouds and my mom said, we have to go back! I asked her why? And said no mommy I don't wanna go back we're gonna make it. But I didn't know how. Then some man had opened his door he was standing in the screen door and shouted hey Ayelle, Ayelle Roberts is that you? My mom shouted back yes who's that? I guess they knew one another cause she and I went all the way up to the door and that's when they both smiled and he looked at me and realized something more was up and he let us into his apt. He had an efficiency apt. A blessing right on time.

He fed us and had given my mom some clothing to put on. How can an uncle say such things when he was raped and touched by the same family members and a great aunt's husband who was a preacher? See there is more to this that they keep quiet. I come from a family of generations of men who rape and sexually abuse the little girls and boys. See I don't know my scriptures word for word verbatim but I surely do read the LORD's words and in the gospel of Haggai:12-14 GOD tells us about unclean priests who claim to be holy, I knew enough to know what was right and wrong as a little girl. I was told that before I was born one of my great aunt's was married to a man who was a local preacher.

This was the man who secretly had ties with the mafia and the masons. Which specific ones I don't know but he had them or shall I say they had him. He was the undercover rapist. He preferred the little boys in the family. To keep the scandal the elders took money and gained property that was not theirs as well as kept it hush hush. I didn't know much about the world but I believed GOD was a good GOD even though I knew very little at that time. What's wrong with this family? See I come from a family who would rather hide the truth than stand up and fight for what's right unless it's street fighting which is very stupid. Stand beside your children! Don't hush up tragic events. Yes sometimes it's better to hide some things but when it comes to the safety of children injustice is not the way!!! Period!

I don't even know the definition of Family….Somebody please help me! I don't know who I am or where I belong? What is my mother to do? GOD why didn't you just let me die on the way out of my mom's tummy? How is my brother or sister? Will they remember me? Are they too being touched? Are they safe? GOD who am I? No one really loves me? All these questions…But no answer just silence. Or so I thought as a child.

Chapter Seven

WE WERE BACKWARDS AND FORWARDS for years until finally my mom decided to start putting her welfare checks in the bank and saving up for a home a real home our home. And that's just what she had done. How I don't know but she did it, we had long struggled extremely hard but my mom had bought her first house and I was just getting ready to turn fourteen!

It was beautiful! All of yard just like we had wanted, three bedrooms, a basement, back porch, front porch, pretty green grass, front room, dining room, kitchen with a sit in table area, and a cat as well as nice neighbors! We were right on same street my mom had grew up on with her brothers and sisters and mom and dad!!! Sharon Line area considered as the country part of town away from the inner part of the city of Youngstown. Mom felt that since her great Aunt had taken her parent's home and would not give back the property to any one of her brothers or sisters that at least she could raise her kids down the street from those memories she used to miss the ones that were good I mean! In case you are wondering I have had to pass over some of these scandalous events done and made by some of my family members!

Even though rightfully I have every right to expose them as well I will leave that judgment to GOD the Father in Heaven and just write more of my life. To this day they even robbed her of the 10 percent of my great grandparent's property on Winton. Somehow they are signing papers and money was taken that no one had a right to all these years.

And no my mom was not a saint trust me! I have issues with a lot of her ways! But all I'm simply saying is if this thing called family would have been just what family is supposed to be, loving, kind, caring and full of joy and laughter, then maybe we as family would have been better and more righteous to one another. But no one wants to admit their wrongs and by the time they do … damage is already done. Even me, instead we point the finger! Never taking responsibility and or remorse for our own actions. This is the flesh of us humans. But I was even blind in this because we are living in the times in which these things were told to happen since the beginning of the original sin.

So we lived in our home a few months but again my heart was troubled because I did not have my siblings. I'll never forget asking my mom to try and regain her custody of them and she was afraid. She said to me if she would try to do this that she will guarantee that we would lose our home! I begged and argued with my mom that she could bring the family back together and he could not keep us separated.

There was a memory of her and I trying to go over there and bring my brother and sister toys and clothes for Christmas when my mom had first got me back home and he wanted to jump on her. She had all new stuff for my brothers and sisters! Two big garbage bags full of gifts and clothes! The only thing she had to put them in. And I remember him taking these bags full of brand new items and throwing them all over the parking lot of

Estate Apartments! The apartment complex he and my siblings lived in with his mother! That broke her heart because he was brain washing them into believing that she did not want them. I remember them crying and screaming and he had not a care of this in the world. My mom was telling me to stop dwelling on these things and that we had a better life now!

But I could not imagine living in this new home without them. I always had this type of heart I could not see anyone I loved hurt, heck I thought we were supposed to love everybody. That people would live in peace and harmony together....Oh the innocence of a child's heart.

That's when my mom finally made the effort to try and regain her custody. He had finally bought the kids over in agreement to talk and they both had decided to let go of their awful past. But we did not know his true intentions. For a few days things were okay but they began to fight and argue. I tried to get along with my brother and sister, but he had taught them that my mother only loved and cared for me so when they would leave the house my brother and sister would always try to do very mischievous things to me.

I tried to tell my mom but their father would say she's just jealous and trying to be grown. For those of you who do not know this form of expression was often used as a term when an adult would say that the child is trying to grow up too fast and wanted to fill the mother's shoes! This was the stupidest expression and I can't stand it to this day because that's when my mother began to abuse me physically, verbally, and mentally. Even though now as a mother myself I understand this meaning but some people abuse words. When he would beat my mother for reasons I can't explain I would just get pissed, I and my siblings would always be begging him to get off of her. To see her after he would beat her face bloody and black and purple eyes.

Swollen face teeth knocked a loose and body bruised! I was truly pissed so I would find things around the house and try to defend my FAMILY! But every time I would do this they would make up and he would say to her... you need to beat her behind! And that's just what she would do. The beatings began, and at first they were with belts, then curtain rods, then hangers, and then the broom, and then the extension cord! Eventually it became her fists and her feet. Kicking me, punching me, pulling my hair! I had no feeling of love as a daughter anymore. My GOD what is happening to me? There is a difference between beating your child out of love and abuse.

It is true what GOD says, Spare the rod spoil the child. Today I can say I witness many young children doing things I would never have been allowed to do. Parents allowing them to basically do whatever they want, because that's what society today teaches us. WRONG! GOD does not say that. GOD teaches obedience and order. GOD himself raises kings and wise men, prophets, and men of righteousness. Abraham, Issac, Moses, Enoch, Isaiah, Solomon, David, Joseph, and most highly praised our LORD and SAVIOR JESUS CHRIST! So I may have had it hard and yes some things went extremely too far, but I understand when it's done the way GOD says to do so.

I would try to put on at least five sweaters and three pairs of jeans when I knew this was coming, but my mom would always say "take em off"! And I would and began to get beaten. One day just before the holidays he beat her, now my brother had asthma very bad and during the process of my mom trying to get him out of the house he tried grabbing my sister but I grabbed her and so he grabbed my brother. We had locked the door but had not realized he got hold of him.

My mom said give me my son and he had my brother on the porch at night refusing to give him to her and saying to my mother you better open the door you B#%&*h! It was freezing cold outside and my brother's asthma was extremely bad then. My mom begged and his father knowing of my brother's condition began just punching my brother in his chest! This man was rotten.

We saw this and began screaming and begging him to stop! He just kept saying open the door B#&%*h! We didn't have a phone anymore at this time. It was disconnected, so we could not phone the police and did not want any more embarrassment so no one ran to a neighbor. Finally my mom opened the door and he said now B#%&*h! You can't get rid of me and there's nothing you can do about it! Your own family dogs you out and no one is going to believe you! I wanted to kill him! Thinking only vengeful and murderous thoughts of wrong doing and unrighteousness.

Thou shalt not kill…. the seventh commandment, but it wouldn't be the last time I ever thought about murder. Reminding me of the truth of how Cain Killed Abel. Of course I cannot compare to actually doing it but the thought is just as worse! I wish I had of read the words GOD spoke of this horrible issue in GENESIS CHAPTER 4 verses 1- 24 before the time I had actually made a murderous attempt. You will hear his words and the more you read his words you will be sure to find that vengeance shall only be his. His judgment is always just. But I was not knowing this until later on in my life. I couldn't do anything. I even started losing my faith in GOD, or so I thought.

I said if GOD was real then why do we suffer like we do? I wondered why I was even on this thing called earth? This evil place? And did I have a purpose? Yes GOD is real, just that I didn't understand. There was still no direction. No one in my family was obedient to him, gave him glory, or worship.

I grew up seeing my family go to church when it was a holiday or when they felt convicted. Praying only when they wanted something instead of every single day and build a relationship with GOD! After that I was on my way to school one day when he was beating her again. I remember just standing there this time wanting to grab a knife and kill him but then remembering how my mother would beat me for jumping in the middle of her fighting him afterwards. These are the evil thoughts that began to spring forth out of my mind.

Since GOD has brought me out and through CHRIST JESUS teaching me, I am still learning how the mind is one of the most favorite places that the devil loves to use as a tool for his wickedness. He has many tricks. That is why it is so important to be shielded by the strength and protection of the LORD JESUS for it was only JESUS who is triumphant in defeating the devil. But I knew this not then, so I just walked out of the door down the street through the path that my mother and her siblings used to take to the Jr. High School that used to be a High School they all once went to.

Chapter Eight

The Beatings

S O I GOT TO SCHOOL and I went into the girls' bathroom and just went into the bathroom stall on the first floor and I cried. I cried so hard about my life and something inside me said just try to concentrate on school today and get to class. As I wiped my face and unlocked the stall door and went to the sink to wash my hands I heard a voice behind me...it was my mother and she said to me you dirty little B#%&*h and pow!

She slapped the mess outta me! She slapped me again and again and again. And I heard a few girls coming into the bathroom but once they saw what was happening they ran out. Surprisingly no one had run and told. I looked at my mom and I asked why? She said to me because you left me while he was jumping on me. I told her, but ma every time I try to jump in and fight for you, you always end up beating on me so I just left. She said you don't ever leave me. Now clean ya d#%n face and go to class... and you better not bring home any F's! I had to walk to class with my face bruised up and red. I'll never forget that.

Then you tell me not to bring home any bad grades. How the heck am I supposed to focus knowing I am living in a house where there is No LOVE! Only hatred, drugs, and abuse. I was faking a smile on the outside but dying on the inside. But no one knew except two besides my brother and sister. My best friend Fiona and Shamilla. They were always there to encourage me when I thought I had no one else. They never judged me when all the other class mates were making fun of me. Alot of the people who I thought were true friends along the way ended up falling off but Fiona has never left my side after 20 years we are still friends to this day.

I was heartbroken. Soon after that I became a real bum in school having to wear high waters and shopless shoes. Only thing I had going for me in school was my makeup. And even then my class mates were clowning the heck outta me because I would draw on my eyebrows to try and look pretty. I used to wear eyeliner on my eyes and lips and still do to this day.

Well not the eyeliner on the lips too much anymore, I finally upgraded to lip liner lol. But I caught hell. They used to call me Snoop Doggy Dog and say that's one ugly girl. Plus my having a jerry curl in the eighth grade after the eighties made me a bigger target. The only real friends I had was Fiona and Shamell! I was what you would call a nerd! I recall having to sell candy to raise money for a trip to Canada in Honors Science.

Well I sold at least one hundred dollars worth of that candy but we had to eat the rest because we ran out of food back at home in my house. My teacher asked me what happened and I said nothing. I think he knew something was wrong but he would never ask. I began to miss school a lot because of what was going on with me at home. The day of the trip I did not go to school. There was a knock at the door and it was my teacher.

He said "where's your mother"? I said she's here and he told me to go get her. So I did, and he said your daughter is very smart and we have this trip to Canada before he could finish my mom said, "I don't have the money". But he said I'll Pay For Her To Go outta my own pocket.

So I looked at my mom and she said that I could go. I told my teacher that I don't have much to wear and he said don't worry about my clothes just get my things and come on. I did this, I packed what little I could for those two days that looked the best and we went to the school. We took a big bus that resembled a greyhound bus but it wasn't. And we were off! We went to New York to see a play on our way there. The year was 1994.

I couldn't believe it. It was people acting out the movie Clue! It was very fun and amazing to me, they were so vibrant and full of life these young actors and actresses. From there we ate and my teacher paid for my food. I was relieved. We entered Canada and I remember some people asking for Birth Certificates and proof of our identity. And we finally got that over with and we were in CANADA! Wow I mean wow!!! We had visited a castle there and it was really historical.

And oh my, my, my when I was on the Maid of the Midst! It was very loud and it sounded like thunder but it was the most magical beautiful thing I had ever seen in my life! See in GENESIS CH1 verses 1-24 GOD created all life and he is surely beautiful and powerful. I just looked at GOD's wonders and all his beauty and I wanted to cry but didn't want anyone to laugh at me in my group. I had had enough of that! These were moments with GOD that I never realized at the time he was showing me that he is Mighty and was with me but then I never understood because I was stuck in my reality back home and begun to block out the things I enjoyed in life due to what I was going through and had been through. Also we went to this very big building and I'm a little afraid of heights but we were some stories up and they had this see through glass floor and beneath us we could see all the cars and people, I was scared to be on that thing lol!

So the trip was over and we journeyed home. It was in the evening and I saw all my other class mate's parents come greeting them with open arms, everyone bragging on the trip but my mom not there. I just slowly went to my teacher and said I'm going to walk home now.

He said well just wait a moment and I told him it was okay I know to walk home. I began to walk through the path thinking man... when I get home what sad feeling or problem will I face? My fun was over, freedom had ended. I opened the door and yelled out to my mother mom I'm home. No response. Kept yelling still nothing. So I dropped my bag and went up in every room up the stairs and basement. My house was empty.

I went to the fridge there was no food. I laid on my mattress and box spring on the floor and just screamed in my pillow wishing that GOD would send an angel to take me home to heaven. I just laid there thinking that I would never treat my kids and family this way and asking myself what I wanted to be when I became an adult? My answer to myself was a Marine Biologist. I never saw that dream. I never even learned to swim, who was I kidding?

My mom returned home. I had questions and one of them was where were you? She explained that my brother, sister, and I didn't have anything to eathave any food so she had to go hustling for food, but I did not expect what she told me next. There was another relative and a certain brother in law of hers who had taken advantage of her while they were drinking. I was extremely upset.

35

Tired of a filthy family plus our home had fallen apart. She was right. He had come and destroyed everything and done exactly what she said he would do. I just cried again. As usual. So I cut and cleaned the chicken she had brought in. Leg quarters. I really don't like leg quarters now lol. We ate those very often, so often I thought I was going to turn into a dang leg quarter. But moving on, I remember also in school one day they had bring your daughter to work day and a few girls were chosen to go to Nation Bank for mentors and women who did not have daughters. And were the best in the class. We had gotten Fresh Mint coins.

And I came home bragging to my mom look what I got. She took my coins to the corner store and sold them for food for us to eat. I was no longer proud and had no more interest in school. No more. This was where I began to believe in nothing and that I would only be like the rest of my family. I felt as if I had no life. But honestly I am now glad about how my life happened. I must sing praises to GOD because you don't have a testimony if you don't go through the test. But back then there was no happiness just emptiness and darkness I thought. I had stopped reading books and writing poetry and just began to listen to music.

Music was my outlet. I would hear the melody of the instruments and song and just imagine being in another place. Like the ocean or on top of a mountain to myself. With only nature and the wind. See I have always had an obsession with nature and the outdoors.

My feet in the grass. The feel of the ocean water flowing through my toes and sand beneath my feet. There was always a feeling to help change the world and a love for fellow humanity. Animals and flowers. Peace and all of GOD'S beauty that he himself took his time to create! Life and love, but this was not my reality. I would often wake up with hunger in my belly and weakness in my heart. Not realizing just how peculiar I was and how fragile I was. I asked GOD often why was I so different and why come I had to go through so much? I was listening to worldly music and not the Gospel or Christian music. Back then I had no real guidance in the LORD.

So music was my way out. Singing only in my bathroom or my bedroom. Sometimes along to songs on the radio and other times to my own words with no music behind me aloud. GOD had given me a gift. I was a singer but had no idea of what blessings GOD bestowed upon me only that I had this voice that everyone said sounded beautiful.

My sibling's dad had gotten his self an apartment in the projects. And was over off and on. He would still beat my mom. We had hell. Back and forth one minute happy next minute hell. I became more and more interested in hell and began thinking GOD did not love me. I would sit in my closet in my room and rock back and forth asking for something to communicate with me and give me answers to my life. I had gotten very dark inside. One day we had went to the south side over to my Aunt Rochelle's house to celebrate because she had just bought her first home. It was fun until my mom said lets go were going home.

I had just gotten a new pair of blue jeans and I purposely left them there because I didn't want to go home to this darkness. We were in darkness because we did not know the LORD! For JESUS said in JOHN CHAPTER 8 VERSE 12, I am the light of the world: he that followeth me shall not walk in darkness, but shall have the light of life. When we got home I told my mom that I had left them there and she said you trying to be grown. It's always you I'm gonna show you something. She hadn't even turned on the lights up stairs and I didn't know what she had grabbed but whatever it was she took that thing and just started hitting me in my room. I began to scream! Begging her to stop, and that's when it happened, I heard a crack like something had broken in my body something wasn't right. She finally decided to stop and turn on the lights and sure enough I had blood dripping from my face. She helped to clean my face and there was a little hole in my nose.

She was beating me with a wooden leg from a chair and it had a nail in it to attach the leg to the chair. My nose was broken. I still have that scar to this day on the left side of my nose.

My heart was broken. Over the night my face had swollen and I believe my nose was broken. My eyes were swollen blue and black and purple, my whole face had swollen up as if I had gotten bitten by a deadly venomous snake or something. My mom could not send me to school like this so I stayed home. I missed at least two or three weeks. I had begun to hate her. One morning my brother and sister were in school and the attendance keeper had come knocking at the door.

My mom had never let him in and he just wanted to know where I was? Why was her child missing so much school? She made up some excuse and just like that he was gone. I healed but not in my heart. I remember being slapped at times, kicked in my back, punched I mean I hated my life!

She left one day and I remember saying to myself this is it...this is my chance to end it all, all I have to do is find some pills, my heart was racing because I was so anxious to find some before she came back. Guess what people? There were only a full bottle of asprin. I was hoping this was enough to end my life. I looked at my sister and brother and said hey, I love you! I'll always love you and don't ever forget that! My sister looked at me and my brother there well there was no way to tell what he was thinking because he would always play in his imaginary world away from his real life.

Meanwhile my little sister would always try to get a little closer to me but I was drifting further and further away from reality myself. See I didn't want to say anything because I knew I could not trust the system and dared not put my siblings through it. Or my mom again so I swallowed those pills and just laid in my bed. When I heard my mom's voice I was extremely afraid to get a whooping. I thought to myself da*n. I was supposed to die before she got back. But NOOO!!! She came in my room and said didn't you hear me calling you? But I was too weak. Not just from the pills but we also didn't have food and that's why she had left to go get something. She saw that I was not really responsive and she began to wonder what was wrong with me? She asked my sister and my sister was scared to answer but once threatened with the belt she finally snitched lol. I had taken those asprin and my mom said OH MY GOD!

She ran downstairs and got that nasty grit form the old cooking grease all of it and had mixed it with melted butter and made me eat it until I vomited all that mess up out of my system. For those of you who don't know what grit is, it's the nasty residue from the chicken or fish cornmeal or flour that's left at the bottom of the skillet. Uggh!

I remember her saying baby you would do this just to get away from me I'm sorry I don't ever want to lose you! But in my mind those words were null and void. Nothing mattered. And then I began to lose who I was. I told one of my uncles about everything that was happening but the real reason he had come to defend anyone was because my siblings dad had made the comment of that's why his son is a paraplegic.

My uncle's son was handicapped and yes he is the same uncle who had abused me. One night as I slept on the couch there was a knock at the door I woke to the sound went to the door and asked who it was? My uncle said who he was and I opened it.

He and one other family member and one other person went running up the stairs. But my brother's and sister's dad was not there yet he didn't get there till the next day.

So my uncle said he would be back and I heard him knocking and let him in. See this night my sibling's dad picked the wrong night to spend the night. I was still downstairs and I heard the thumping and rumbling. Soon as I knew it here comes my uncle dragging their dad down the steps and had beat him in the face with his pistol. My mom and I and siblings just stood and couldn't believe it. I was full of hatred for what this man was doing to my mother, brother, and sister and this alone made me feel no compassion for him. To me he was getting exactly what he deserved for the heartaches and injustice we had to endure.

I kept hearing my mom begging him to stop saying that's enough. STOP IT STOP IT! They had thrown him out and he got his clothes on and left. For once he had learned what it felt like to be humiliated in front of your children and hurt. I thought it was over. He never bothered my brother and sister again and we were okay for a little while. But one day we were all gone over a family member's house for a few days because my mom was afraid. Upon our return we saw that all of the aluminum siding off the house was torn completely off.

My mom unlocked the door to find that our walls were damaged things were broken everywhere and when we went in the basement we saw that he had busted all of our pipes and water was everywhere flooded and frozen because it was winter.

He had come and destroyed our home. We were nowhere near paying off that loan our home was home no more. We lost the house and we had no choice but to leave and this time my brother and sister was there. We ended up losing our house and my mom begged my grandmother to come back and live with her for a while because the state was threatening to take us away because they deemed the house condemned. She told her no and my mom had no choice but to ask my friend's dad if we could rent a room just to lay our heads.

I hated that time because this too was not the best. There were men and women coming in and out of the house everyday all day due to the fact that most of the people living there were on crack cocaine. But my mother did what she had to do to try and keep her children even if that meant having to lay down her pride.

My mother's heart was broken and she blamed me for it all! Sometimes she would say things like she should've just killed me, don't look at her, nobody wants me, and I'm the reason her life was messed up. I had become more and more withdrawn even to myself.

Chapter Nine

MOM DECIDED TO JUST GO and move and live with a relative in California, so she bought four Greyhound tickets to Cali. I was scared but happy to get out of the hell at home. So we left. And we were greeted with open arms. See out west at my new school no one made fun of me I had one friend named Sandra. And my cousin and I cousin were as close as ever there. He always had my back and I had his! I had never seen kids whose parents had so much money for their families and most of the teenagers had cars! They would kick it like something out of the movies even though we were out in the country area! I had begun drinking and smoking weed. But never had been that much of a weed fan. I loved my cousins, admired Miche because of her beauty and intelligence. I loved them all very much because of the love and warmth I had not received back home.

But that ended pretty bad too and we left not only because of disagreements but also my grandmother had gotten very ill. This is where I found out that heart problems, diabetes, and cancer runs heavily in my family especially in the women so back to Youngstown we went! I hated every minute of living back there. It would start off as a family barbecue and end in someone calling the police. No knowledge of generational curses. LORD GOD to help me explain. Generational curses are upon you when you have no idea of why it seems likes everything in your life or that you touch is sour.

Well because since the beginning of our creation man was separated from GOD because he rebelled and did as the LORD told him not to do. GENESIS CH 3 verses 1-24. You may want to read this. See satan himself had rebelled against GOD and he as well as 1/3 of the angels who followed him were cast out of heaven. Satan hates us and he is deceiving people into worshipping him every day even still. So generational rebellion through this first act of sin from generation to generation still go on. You must be saved through JESUS and ask him to break these things from your life, casting down every unclean thing and every spirit of darkness satan will throw at you. Become spiritually strong though GOD'S WORDS by reading your bible and staying in prayer.

Read also the book of ISAIAH and DANIEL as well as JEREMIAH. GOD has many great prophets he left his word to that he knew we would need to guide us through life because of this. It is truly spiritual warfare and we can't win without JESUS for he was, is, and will always be victorious! I didn't have any idea then and that is why GOD says teach your children his ways, will, and righteousness. JESUS spoke truth. The books of MATTHEW, MARK, LUKE, JOHN and his words are everlasting and eternal. The apostles knew this. Paul was to me one of the greatest because of all our GOD has shown and given him! I'm still learning. Even I don't know the bible word for word or can quote scripture and know exactly where it is but I know from experience it is GOD'S TRUTH!!

Now I didn't want to return because of all the times we were rejected by family back at home and I wanted to see us make it in California but before I knew it we were back again at square one. We ended up moving in with my grandma and also my aunt Rochelle and her kids because she too needed somewhere to go with her kids as well and had tried leaving out west as well but just a different state.

So we all needed somewhere to go. I enrolled at Raven Score High School. I hated going there because I had the same problems I was having at my old school before we left. I still had a Jerri Curl in my hair and my clothing was not always the hottest and latest fashions. Aunt Nicole was supposed to be the boss of everyone who stayed there because one she was the oldest and two she had helped co- sign for my grandmother's house. Funny thing is everyone was paying rent to my grandmother but her mortgage was never paid? Hmmm?

My uncle stayed there, my mom and her kids, aunt and her kids, and youngest aunt. So where was the money going everybody was giving? Made no sense but supposedly we never paid. Everybody had something to say but never would stand up and say anything about it. The only one who really would argue with everybody would be my mom and we would always end up getting put out. Then once again my mom met a guy, his name was Borus.

Or so I had thought. Little did I know that this was an old high school sweetheart of hers that was actually a crack addi in disguise. He convinced my mom to move into a house on the east side of town and she moved him in. He was on crack cocaine and he too began abusing my mother. This did not sit well with me and here we go again I was jumping in the fights.

I would sometimes spend the night over my Aunt Nicole's house to get to school on the north side because this is where she lived. And her oldest two daughters and I were the same ages. I sometimes would ask to borrow some of my cousin's clothes and shoes just so I wouldn't get laughed at as much in school but she would always say no and sometimes even act like I was not her cousin in school.

I guess she felt embarrassed at times that I was because she was popular in school. And her sister who was the more heavier and darker one was a little popular only because of being her sister. Funny thing though is whenever someone would even think that they would just fight one of my cousins I would be the first to approach the situation even if that meant getting my butt kicked but I couldn't even borrow a pair of socks? But I always looked over it. I began to run away from home and skip class. Mainly math class because I felt like I was dumb and couldn't get past division. But you give me any other subject and it was on !I remember letting my cousin cheat off my English homework when she noticed I was getting straight A's in all my subjects except mathematics and that's when she asked. But when I asked to use her cheat sheet for math her friend had given her she would always tell me no.

I remember going to the mall with them and having no money and one of them bought me some food at the food court. While they were hanging out with friends I was walking alone and met a guy. He told me he was eighteen and I bought it. He was sooo attractive. His name was Tevonte. Tevonte was very muscular with a caramel complextion, and hazel eyes. His teeth we're pretty shade of pearl white with beautiful smile with smooth brown lips. He said I was pretty and told me to call him but I knew that I was not allowed to talk to boys but I ended up calling him a week later. I remember being at home and asking my mom about sex while she was bathing. She slapped the mess outta me. And said I better not think about it. She said that I was hot in the behind and going to be a little whore. Now GOD tells us in Proverbs using King Solomon as the vessel that the tongue is the sword and careful what we let come from our lips through our tongue. There is power as well as much foolishness that comes from loose lips. PROVERBS 15 verses 1-33 speaks a lot about the tongue.

I ran away for the first time to the South side over an older cousin's house I always wanted to be like her just because she was high yellow with long hair and all the boys liked her. She was older than me but very pretty. See I was dealing with an identity crisis because of how I was always mistreated and felt the need and want to be accepted. I told her about everything and she said any time I wanted to come over that she would never tell on me. And that's when I called Tevonte. We talked on the phone for a little bit and he wanted to come get me but I would not let him. I went over to the North side back over to my aunt's and called him again. You're probably wondering what I was thinking? Well I was thinking I'm a virgin and a good girl, but if I was going to get slapped for doing things I never really was, then I may as well just do it. This could not have been one of my most stupidest thoughts of negativity I have ever done but it wouldn't be the last. It did start the one out of the various excuses from my anger in doing things I used to call getting back at people who hurt me. But really I was just repeating a generational pattern and digging myself into a ditch of darkness.

I would say things like, my dad does not love me. My mom hates me and no matter what I do she never appreciates me for being a good girl. I always felt as if I needed that approval in my life as well as other peoples. The moment I asked her about sex she slaps me? I may as well say forget it and do it! Yes people I lost my way. I told my cousins I was going to call him and leave out for a while and they promised not to tell.

Chapter Ten

Unpure....

NOW I WAS THINKING THAT your first time was supposed to be sweet and magical. I thought he was going to love me forever. And marry me. DUMMY CARD BIG TIME! He took me to a motel and this man performed oral sex on me. At first I was freaking out and said what are you doing? He said just relax.

It's cool trust me you'll like it. Just lay back. I'm not gonna hurt you. So I laid back and he proceeded again. It was wet and uncomfortable. I just laid there waiting for the moment that it would start feeling good...but it never did.

I had missed something. All I knew was that I had finally done it out of anger towards my life. Well when he finished he said to me that I was not a virgin that I had to be lying about being a virgin in the first place, but I thought he was crazy. I didn't understand why he said this but I just left it alone because I had never been willingly touched before him. Remember my past.

He also revealed to me that he was twenty one and not eighteen. This devastated, me all my life older men had taken advantage of me and once again I was hurt. But I still thought he cared about me. I was wrong.

He took me back to my aunt's home. There was no kiss goodnight... just I'll call you. I just got out. I went in the house and my Aunt still was not off work yet. My cousins were there and it's funny, even though my cousin and I had our difference she always knew me very well. So she asked me if I had done it? I tried to lie but I've never been too good at it. So she knew and well I eventually just fessed up. She and her sister were all tripped out and asking me how was it? What did it feel like? What did it look like? Honestly it was a pretty ugly looking thing lol. But I thought it would change me for some reason? Guess what? It did but not like I had wanted it to. It made me even more confused about myself, my body, my sexuality, and men.

After that they became tadle tells but you knew that was coming. Eventually Antie got off work and yes that scary question came and I admitted it. She did to this day what I would've done if it was my niece. TELL HER MOTHER! But at the time I was scared to death!

My mom found out and I just kept running for a while but I went home. And my mom kicked my butt but it wasn't as bad as I thought it would be. So I kept in school but still I skipped out on school due to the harassment of the other students about how ugly they thought I was or my clothes and shoes. Plus I was embarrassed that I knew next to no math but I was very smart in every other subject.

This was way too embarrassing for me. So I began skipping and running the streets when I should've had my behind in class! I didn't know that children could be so cruel. But it's even worse today. I don't know their life story but some are struggling and some have made it. I can forgive them now. We all make mistakes. For JESUS said in MATTHEW Chapter 12-15 forgive and ye shall be forgiven.

But I do realize that I let my fears scare me away from becoming the Marine Biologist I should've been and the humanitarian I wished to become. GOD is not the author of fear, shame on me! So when I was attending class I got word that Tevonte, the guy I had given my virginity to, had not only gotten to me but was going out with and having sex with girls from Warren city high schools, Boardman, Austintown, Akron, and all the schools on the North, South, East, and West side of Youngstown Ohio! That's just what running after the spirit of lust and fornication will get you. Embarrassment, a broken heart, early pregnancy, and sometimes even disease! I KNOW!! See I'm not ashamed to tell you so that you will not make the same mistakes by not following the LORD JESUS. Thank you LORD I never got stricken with herpes, Aids, or Hepatitis. Wait on GOD teenagers, he will see you through and wants you to be happy!

I was heated angry. Because I thought that a guy gets a girls virginity and chooses to be with her and her only. I thought they practiced safe sex and if nothing else at least just have sex with the one girl you have been with not EVERYBODY! But again how innocently stupid I was at the time. I didn't even understand myself or my life so how was I to understand this world or the ignorance in it? Heck I was a part of it. I just didn't understand the blessings in being a virgin. That it is truly a high and righteous honor in the sight of the LORD! Even though mines was horribly defiled as a child, this was no excuse to run out and do what I did, because in my spirit when committing this act. I knew it was not right inside of me. That this was not truly what I wanted to do.

But I had a dumb and bad habit of acting in anger or hurt. This is the easiest way the devil can squirm his way in, by the open nooks and crannies of your emotions. The very reason why we must stay in prayer and faith in our LORD JESUS for strength and guidance. Because we can be often times very ignorant. Well I can admit to mines.

So we moved in an apartment on the Northside on Elm Street. Ugh I know huh? But yes it was just what comes to mind with the street title A Night mare. We had just some beds and some clothes. My brother and sister were going to Haykes Jr. High and they were having it just as hard in school as I was. I wanted to do something but I could do nothing. One day after school I had gotten the two forms that every teenager gets at sixteen. One form was to learn to drive and the other to work.

Chapter Eleven

Black Out

I KNEW THAT MY MOM had not one dime for my driving so I didn't even worry over that. But the form that was most important was the one for the job. I asked her to fill it out and I said mom if I get a job this will help us out a lot. I got tired of getting laughed at because of my clothing as well as my siblings dealing with the same thing I wanted to provide for us. I know it wouldn't be a whole lot but something is better than nothing. I couldn't believe what came next. She said to me,

"If you get a job then that will cut down our check every month. Oh I'm not going to sign it. But when you get eighteen you can." What the heck did you just say I thought. This made absolutely no sense? Money through the whole month verses money every 1st of the month? I thought you wanted me to be different than you? I thought you wanted me to make it? All those questions I wanted to ask but I knew not to. I blamed her for everything. But I just didn't understand that life and family members had beaten her down mentally, men and relationships, drinking and drugging.

Again that's why GOD says don't judge others because some lose sight of things and don't realize what they do. I now know she just had no sense of direction anymore. So I left well enough alone. I started hanging out with my best friend since first grade who stayed only a few blocks away. She was going through some pretty heavy stuff herself! She was always so pretty and so smart and she had a smile that could light up a room. I always knew she would make it. She now works for the government and brings in some pretty good bucks a year! I'm so proud of her.

I started going over there because I felt at peace and her mom was trying to start over and had found GOD. Her mom was a piece of work too almost if not just as bad as mines but her mom was in search of the love to find Jesus. And she found him thank you Jesus. Now as I myself have found him I understand why the LORD says do not return to old life and people you used to be around. It's not that you think that your better it's just that GOD means what he says and wants you to live righteously and even if that means you have to let go of your closest relatives so be it. For his is better than anything or anyone in this world can offer you.

And that's real LIFE! She too has a story to tell but I am not going to get into her life. I don't have that right. Over there I got to talk to my best friend and she would tell me how she felt just as I would tell her how I felt just like when we were little. I remember turning seventeen years old and I spent my birthday over her house and went to church with her mom and her siblings. I felt good. I also remember she would mime to her church songs and my favorite was He'll Never Put More On Me Than I Can Bare! For some reason the words from this particular song uplifted me, as well as the song Order My Steps In Your Word! But when I went home my mom was pissed. Again satan had entered my heart every time I got home through all the hurt and pain. I never looked to pray as much as I should have because I would be angry and distracted by what I was living.

I arrived and she had made me a chocolate cake. I said thank you and was happy but disappointed. Because after all these years of being my mom you forgot I hate chocolate cake and don really eat icing? So the fact that the icing was chocolate was even worse. She saw this disappointment in me and started cursing. Calling me ungrateful and asked where I had been? When I told her where this angered her more because of a past story I can't let you in on. But she knew that what secret that was being hidden was wrong.

So she slapped me and told me to cut the cake. One of the worst birthdays ever because this man was there. And sometimes he seemed as if he enjoyed seeing my mom slap and hit me. Sometimes I would even hear him say BEAT HER ASS…she's always trying to be grown, she act like she's the mother and you're the child. Like she running sh@t baye. And this would only Egg my mother on and she would do just that…beat me and I hated him with a passion. I began hating men more and more.

I cried myself to sleep that night. And sometimes I would look out the window when I woke up and just wonder if I jumped out the window and just ended my life would I go to heaven?(murderous spirit) But I knew that suicide was a sure ticket to hell and this I did not want. I did not always fall asleep in church when we did go. And surprisingly my mom used to know her bible very well! So I knew of JESUS a little she just didn't explain a lot to me nor did we read together. I just didn't know why my life was like this? After that I hung out over my girl's house around the corner a lot more after school. She also knew everything I was going through. But praise is not just something you need to do in church. You should and can praise JESUS IN YOUR OWN HOME!

53

So my old friend was from Connecticut and moved to my city. Her name was Elicia. She encouraged my running lol she would say girl hell keep running! And she knew that I had the biggest crush on Sky! He was always such a gentleman nice, and well-dressed mannered, and sweet but I was just too shy to say anything and so was he. One day at school I decided to ask him out. But he said he had to think about it...so I had taken that as a no. He, I, and my friend had drama class together and I actually liked drama class a little so I would go. One day I came to class with a black eye and some girls were making fun of me for it. My girl saw that this was pretty much going to make me snap and she was right because when I did no one knew it was coming except her.

She hugged me and I left the school because I felt this uncontrollable urge of anger. I got really drunk and came home really late after hanging out over my cousins on the south side. I was a little good at hiding that because my mom didn't really pay me any attention after a while when the man named Borus came into her life.

I went to the kitchen and grabbed a butcher knife and put it under my pillow because I said to myself enough is enough! My brother and sister were asleep. I soon fell asleep. The next thing I knew my baby sister and brother were yelling and my sister had run in the room shaking me saying wake up Elisheva! I asked what was wrong and my little sister then told me his man was beating on our mother. Now honestly I didn't give a damn anymore but my sister kept saying please get up! So I finally got up and walked into the living room.

This man had my mother by the throat and was punching her in her face and stomach. I saw my little brother trying to stop it but he pushed him and told him he would beat his ass and then my sister was screaming. I begged him to let go of our mother but he wouldn't and then my sister ran over and tried to pull him off of our mother…he pushed her….from that moment I SNAPPED! I began to talk out loud to myself on the way to my room and I said I done told this son of a b#tch to keep his hands off of my family and I asked him nicely! I said since men like to beat on women I'm about to beat on a man! I grabbed the butcher knife from under the pillow and I ran back into the living room and I screamed out the words YOU MOTHER FUCKIN B#%CH I TOLD YOU TO STOP!

And after that everything went black. I could hear nothing for a short while and then I heard the voice of my mother saying baby that's enough baby stop! STOP! I looked and he was standing there holding his chest and there was blood everywhere! He began to slide down the wall and ask my mom to help him and call 911! I dropped the knife and I couldn't believe my eyes… What have I done? This is why I cannot judge anyone for JESUS our GOD said himself in John chapter 8 verse 7, He that is without sin among you, let him cast the first stone. Many times I still find myself even to this day falling short of the glory of our LORD by making this mistake. For only GOD his self is judge and I often find myself in repentance when confessing my wrong in prayer when I sin in any way before the LORD. The one thing that keeps me going is his spiritual food to the soul which is showing me and still teaching me the way. I find that I am often very opinionated, and GOD with his highly righteous and beautiful COMFORTER always reminds me that I must stay in my place. For no man is higher than GOD nor is he to judge. One of the best things about being saved by JEHOVAH'S love and grace is that he already knew we couldn't make it without for all have sinned and come short of his glory. When we make mistakes we can be corrected by JESUS and he will forgive us. Now that doesn't mean for us to just do things intentionally that are unrighteous or just keep on making those same mistakes! But it does mean that GOD is well aware of our many foolish actions and this is why he came down here on earth in the flesh himself to save our poor pitiful souls for he already knew we could not and would not make it to heaven without him!!

So at that time in my life of ignorance I thought to myself, what did I do? Am I going to go to jail for the rest of my life? Look at all this blood? Is he okay? I mean I know I hated him but I said to myself you've lost it you've really lost it this time! I began screaming and crying and my mom, well she took that knife from me and ran out of the apartment. I remember running to go get him a towel and trying to stop his bleeding. I didn't know how severe his wounds were. To this day my mom has never told me what she did with that weapon. She called the police and one officer began to question me upon arrival.

He knew I was afraid. This officer asked me what happened and I told him. He said that because those to had a history of fighting that I was not gonna go to jail like I thought. But I never got arrested or anything? Well except juvenile when I was hanging out with my cousin and her friends when they were stealing and me being with them the big dummy who carried the merchandise out of the shopping center. Thou shalt not steal! But anyways, I don't know why and neither did my mom. I now know that GOD'S grace was truly upon me and still is for us all! My mom went to the hospital with him.

The next day when she got back from the hospital she talked to me very nicely and said she loved me. She told me that what I had done was wrong and that he decided not to press charges because of her and she was very grateful! She said that his stab wounds were in his heart, his ribs, and his lungs. I could've killed him and it was the grace of GOD that he was okay. I felt some sense of relief because he made it through. I was not a murderer! What was happening was that murderous spirit had entered into me and

I didn't realize that could even exist. But I was glad that he did not die. Thank you JESUS I thought! A week or two had passed and my mom seemed nicer and it seemed like everything was gonna change. Like this opened her eyes and I had my mom back!

Wrong. A few days later I heard the door to the apartment open and I heard my mom's voice and another set of footsteps. It was my mom and the man she loved! She had let him back in. He used this unfortunate event to make her feel as if she owed him something. I started to go to my room when my mom said no, you stay right there and he sat down. My mom looked at me and said you thought you were gonna get away with that? I'm getting ready to beat your ass! And believe me when I say she did! Before I knew it I was being punched and slapped in my face, hair pulled out, and kicked. I was kicked in my stomach a few times, drug across the floor by my hair and punched and slapped in my face. This all happened while he sat and watched her do it. There were so many demonic spirits present in and around my life that almost everything was going hay wire. See what I did not understand was that in life you have to read GOD'S WORDS in order to see what's really happening around you. Years of staying brain washed up under the spell of the television and listening to the media and music I thought I was drowning out my reality, but didn't realize until GOD THIS PAST YEAR has been showing me and teaching me the truth since I accepted JESUS CHRIST AS MY LORD AND SAVIOR! Spirits jump in and out of people every day. The music we listen to that we really think makes us feel good, the thing we allow our families to watch. Oh and let's not forget about the materialistic things and the idol worship. THIS IS A MAJOR ONE TO GOD! That cannot be stressed enough. Most important one of all, EXODUS CH 1 VERSE 1 and GOD spoke all these words: I AM THE LORD YOUR GOD, WHO BROUGHT YOU OUT OF EGYPT IN THE LAND OF SLAVERY. YOU SHALL HAVE

NO OTHER god's BEFORE ME. YOU SHALL NOT MAKE UNTO YOURSELVES ANY GRAVEN IMAGE IN THE FORM OF ANYTHING IN HEAVEN ABOVE OR ON THE EARTH BENEATH OR IN THE WATERS BELOW. YOU SHALL NOT BOW DOWN TO THEM OR WORSHIP THEM: FOR I, THE LORD YOUR GOD, AM A JEALOUS GOD, PUNISHING THE CHILDREN FOR THE SIN OF THE FATHERS TO THE THIRD GENERATION OF THOSE WHO HATE ME, BUT SHOWING LOVE TO A THOUSAND GENERATIONS OF THOSE WHO LOVE ME AND KEEP MY COMMANDMENTS.

Chapter Twelve

Idolatry and false worship....

W E ALL HAVE DONE THIS one. Lovers of money, clothes, cars, men, women and so on and so forth. As soon as one of the popular celebrities come out with some new thing everyone else thinks it's cool. But what we didn't know was that some of many celebrities have sold their souls for the price of these things. They just won't tell us about this! Because we as people just view what we watch and hear as the truth. They have been flashing this fact in our faces for years but no one would even notice including me. Meanwhile they with the devil would laugh at us and say WHAT FOOLS, THEY ARE EATING RIGHT OUT OF OUR HANDS! Even right now as we speak more and more laws are being passed to take away our rights and our freedom of speech and right to bear arms. Fabricating the truth behind what's really going on that a lot of these school shootings and so called mysterious bombings are planned. And it's just not happening here but around the world too many of GOD'S CHILDREN. Look at the 70,000 men women and children who were killed in Syria. SMH! GOD himself sees this and even said he is angered with his many of his children because of this. In HOSEA CHAPTER 4:1 Hear the word of the LORD, YE CHILDREN OF ISRAEL: for the LORD hath a controversy with the inhabitants of the land, because there is no truth, nor mercy, nor knowledge of GOD in the land.

By swearing, and lying, and killing, and stealing, and committing adultery, they break out and blood toucheth blood. VERSE: 6. My people are destroyed for lack of knowledge: because thou hast rejected knowledge, I will reject thee, that thou shalt be no priest to me: seeing thou hast forgotten the law of thy GOD, I will also forget thy children. Now I don't know about you but this scares me. The reason why is because GOD speaks to you when you read his word. I too once partook in this harlotry. Hearing GOD speak through his HOLY WORD I knew I had to submit myself to his will because I wanted to truly follow CHRIST and not be one of many left behind. No man, no one can go against GOD. We all know that GOD sees everything but when you really start understanding that nothing goes unseen, and all this crap about evolution and people forming from ape to human on our somehow mysterious own and then you WAKE THE HECK UP BY LISTENING TO GOD, you SNAP OUT OF IT! GOD IS TALKING, and THIS IS THE REAL DEAL. Of course GOD told me to keep reading to understand about being saved by the grace of JESUS when you except him into your heart and believe in how he, meaning JESUS, shed his precious blood on the cross for you and I. But I again due to lack of knowledge I too did not know.

So that is just a touch to you on unseen things and lack of knowledge on my end as well. But I was still blind not knowing what entities were roaming around in our lives. Then the boyfriend who kept smiling and saying things to encourage my mom to abuse me just got a kick of excitement through it all. By the time she was finished with me, I was completely sore and bleeding from my face. That's when I said GOD...I can't be here anymore and I never want to see her again. I waited until she sent me to school the next day. I went to class and I told Mrs. Wilis I was dropping out. She finally was the one adult I told and she looked as if this broke her heart. She was watching me even when I didn't know she was this whole time.

Chapter Thirteen

Had to Break Away

S HE EVEN TOOK ME TO the guidance counselor's office to show me my grades when I am in school and not surprised everyone except math was an A or B maybe a C lol but actually not a bad report card. Math was my D.

They asked was I sure this was what I wanted to do? After all this is me throwing away my future. But I felt I had no choice. I'm not going back into the hands of the state or into the hands of my mother. I thought to myself. They hugged me and I hugged them and just like that I never got to earn my High School Diploma or go to Prom. I was gone. I went home but I waited until dark because I had to make up a lie about going over my one friend's house for a while. And I left and said I'll be back.

She said okay. And I kissed my brother and sister told them I loved them and I left. I stopped over my one friend's house down the street and she said well if you're gonna go I'm going too. Her name was Layla. I said to her girl you crazy plus you're gonna get into trouble. Her life sucked too, from all the things she had told me, even though I tried to convince her to stay home, my home girl just refused to have that and after looking around at the dark I kind of said ya know what?

Maybe having her with me won't be such a bad idea. So she went in her apartment and just like that she came out and we were gone.

Now the both of us didn't know not one thing about what we were doing but JESUS walked with us alot of cold nights without us knowing he was there. The one night she took me to like a cousin's house of hers and we ate and spent the night there. We left there though and was just street walking sometimes all times of the night. I forgot alot of the memories but we were always finding some young dudes to kick it with and we would smoke weed and drink.

Guys would try to get some sex but I wouldn't do anything because I was still scary with giving it up. But my home girl well I love that crazy lady! We thought we were having fun because we were dealing with back at our homes. It was like we were free but after a few nights we realized we needed somewhere to live and some food and clothes man where were we gonna get this stuff from?

So she knew a lady on the south side and she had two kids. So we went there and told her what was going on and how we were not gonna go back but needed a place to stay. She was very nice and told us as long as we watched her kids she wouldn't snitch us out, she was cool for taking us in but she was a trip to live with. We did this and for clothes we would go down to the goodwill on certain days and got the cutest clothes we could find and shoes and turn them into something. If you didn't know what we were going through you just didn't know we were as poor as we were. And thinking we had all the answers.

Now we would keep the kids and leave when she would come back, we would have the rest of the night to ourselves and we would car hop. Just go chill with some dudes and leave. Half those guys I don't even remember. I would get numbers I wouldn't even call. Only smoke their weed and drink and leave but the dudes were cool about it! Oh how young and inexperienced I was.

One night there was this one time we decided to pull this little car hoping junk and got in with these two dudes. We got to their hang out spot and realized it was a dope house. I was very afraid. The guy who was trying to talk to me told me to come upstairs with him, I said no I don't wanna leave my friend and he said to me she good…she's a big girl, I just wanna holla at you.

So I looked at her and she said it's cool girl we just gonna talk so I said okay and followed him upstairs. Once we got upstairs I noticed graffiti in red spray paint and I knew what that meant. He said come here and sit on the bed next to him and turned off the lights. He asked me was I a virgin and I said no but I don't just go around having sex either and he said well you gonna have sex with me. I said no I didn't feel comfortable and he said Oh you gonna give me some! I just thought to myself don even fight this dude, he is bigger than you, you may as well just do it get it over with and make it outta this house alive, because he didn't look right at this moment and I didn't know what he was gonna do. From that day forward after that experience I didn't car hop anymore. My friend did her thing and I just didn't feel like car hoping was cool. I learned my lesson.

Chapter Fourteen

Heartache On Top Of Pain

W E MADE IT OUT AND we were safe. It wasn't until one night at the lady's house when we were outside I remember someone saying. What's up across the street from us and she said something back. Then we were invited over later on to play cards. So later on we went over and when I walked in I saw one cute guy out of the three who were there. Come to find out he was the eldest brother of the jerk who kept clowning on me and my friend with his funny looking high yellow self and big ole nose but he was a little skinny cutie to me for some reason. I always had the corniest jokes. I could never roast back. But I didn't know that it would be the big nosed one would be the one who would always have my heart.

It became very often that he and I would hang out and my home girl hung out with his friend. I remember him trying to kiss me and I would say I don't kiss. When really I didn't know how to. But when he kissed me with those big ole lips it was the nicest feeling on my neck. He took his time and he knew I was scared. He was very gentle and I felt like I had finally truly lost my virginity even though I knew he was not the first he sure felt like it. After that it was like I couldn't hardly wait to see him. I just knew he was the one. We would talk about making it out of Youngstown and he told me I should go back to school and I agreed.

One day around the holidays I began to miss my family and I stopped over my Aunt Rochelle's home on the Southside. I told her I loved her and missed the family. She just tried to get me to come in but I didn't want anyone to know it was me and that I stopped by. But you know Christmas is one of those holidays where the meaning of love is supposed to be expressed.

I kind of wanted my mom to think I was dead. And my aunt said baby your mother is worried about you. She loves you, I know you don't think so but she does. Where are you staying? I felt bad and told her but asked her not to tell. She said okay and asked if we were hungry but we said no and left. My best friend said I was an idiot of coarse she was gonna tell my mom. But my guilt couldn't let me stay silent, I couldn't lie to my aunt about something like that. I had been gone for a two months.

So we went back to the lady's house and we slept. Well what do you know the next day I saw my mom. She said she loved me and missed me. She caught me turning a corner down the street from where we were staying. She said she was sorry but I didn't care. She said that since I didn't want to come home that she would talk to the lady about me staying there and I think she was paying her like fifty bucks per month for me to stay and my mom began giving me 100 dollars just so I will be okay out there and not broke.

So I began to stay there. One evening I was visited by the young man who I thought stole my heart and he began to ask me what

I had thought about the military? He was asking this because he had a daughter and he was selling vacuums for a living along with drugs to make a living for his daughter. He said he had grown tired of doing this because he didn't want to miss out on her childhood due to the risk of being incarcerated. This I could understand because my dad had not been there for me and even though I did not want to lose him I loved him so I would rather him choose to make an honest living for his child than to be selfish and try to hold on to him. So I was happy for his decision of the NAVY and hurt at the same time. I felt as if he was my first and was to be my last. But we all change, he changed, and I well....I lost me before I even knew who I was. Sadness was beginning to turn into silent rage, I just didn't know it.

I of course had no kids at the time and felt very alone but the choice was if you love someone you make the decision to let them go only hoping they will not forget about you and come back to you. I was wrong again only about him ever coming back.

So soon he had left. And again I felt all alone. My stay at the lady's house had ended, due to an argument I can't even remember. So from there I went back only by the agreement I could live with my grandmother and my mom began to pay her for my stay there. I could always stay as long as there was money. Which soon became hell to me again because my family would always fight one another...as usual.

They were compulsive drinkers and there were other issues that all of us as children were unaware of at that time. But these issues would soon come into the light. So I would still get phone calls from the gentleman while staying with my grandmother. This made me very delighted until one day I got the call he had met a girl. And he had bought her a tennis bracelet? What? I was highly pissed because this was the guy who I had loved even though we were not officially together he had my heart.

That was the official beginning of my own downfall because I cried so hard and became so frozen with this that I just lost hope and didn't care. Still I lost out on love. It would soon become a consistent thing for me to try and give my heart dry to show my affection for people. So my friend had to go back to her family because my grandmother said she was not going to harbor a minor. In which I understood.

Everyone had begun saying that my mom and I along with my siblings were just trouble. I tried to get back into school but the only transportation for kids who had dropped out at the time was a special education bus and after being laughed at so many times for riding on the special bus I had decided to not return again. I guess you could say I had developed the habit of being sheltered in my own little world. So humble in heart that I truly could not face alot of evil even my own. But if I had known what I know now I would've said to heck with what everyone else thinks!

Months later I was standing outside and noticed that this old man up the street was staring down the street at me all of the time. And not just at me always also whenever my family would get to drinking and fighting it would be almost like watching an action movie. And this was also very embarrassing for me. I thought he was a very creepy old man. It got so bad that one day I just ran out of my grandmother's house while it was raining I mean pouring down hard! And I had on no coat nor had an umbrella but I didn't care about that I just wanted to get out! While walking and getting drenched I saw this black two door cougar with a burgundy rag top pull up next to me driving very slowly and this same old guy from up the street and he said, "so are you gonna just keep looking stupid walking in the rain"?

Chapter Fifteen

Becoming Numb

OR ARE YOU GONNA LET me give you a ride? I turned and asked "what the f#ck are you here for?" And he said look i'm just trying to help. Now you could either keep walking in the rain, or just get in the car out of the rain. It's up to you....so eventually I got into the car. This guy asked me if I was hungry and I said yes. He said what would you like? I said I guess KFC. So there we went. He asked me what was bothering me and said he always sits and watches what's going on down there and that I looked like I needed someone to talk to.

He was so right. We went back to his house and we just talked. He offered me some liquor and before I knew it I was getting toasted with the creepy old guy up the street. And he was so funny and made me laugh alot. From then on his place I believed at the time was my safe haven away from my reality.

I felt safe for the moment. I had eaten and had a few drinks. And thank the Lord he was not a murderer cause come to think of it...

that was pretty stupid of me to just trust anybody but I had the habit of just running by that time. And God was the one who was truly with me! I just didn't know it.

I left and was questioned about where I had been? I made up some story that I was over this young man's house I had met. And before I knew it I was going to his house all of the time. But I would always have to go in the evenings. One evening he offered to take care of me, he saw I needed clothes and he said that he would start giving me money and that he liked me. He asked me if he could kiss me? I was very afraid, I was not used to the touch of a man this old. He was 42 at least that's what he had told me. And what about my baby?

The guy that I had still loved? But my heart turned cold and reminded me that this young man I believed in had forgotten about me, that he was enjoying his life with the girl he had bought the tennis bracelet for, and that I once again I had been let down. He would not return to me and marry me like I had wanted. So I kissed the man. His hands had started on my legs. He knew nothing about making love. We ended up in his bedroom and that's where he entered my body with and I was no longer afraid of him.

I felt as if I belonged to him.

Again I was wrong. Often I had to come to him in the night because he had a woman. Eventually he told me and I was not happy with this but he explained that I could still do all the things I was before him and he would still keep me happy. This sounded good but only thing is I could never bring myself to mess around with any guys my age because I felt like I was his. I didn't want to be untrue. So I had my fun but would not sleep around. One day I realized I had not had a period. I was scared to death of what my mother and family would say hoping I wasn't pregnant.

If so how am I going to tell my mom? I had become a drop out, had not went to college, and had no money. Was I pregnant? My mom had taken me to the emergency because she noticed I was always eating and vomitting and I was gaining a few pounds. It came back that I was pregnant....OMG! My mom looked at me and asked by who? I had to tell her how old he really was. I couldn't even look her in the face. But I had to and so I did. She was furious and disappointed. She said she wanted to meet him. So went over there. He was sweating badly and offered my mom a drink. They both looked at me and said what do you want to do? How dare they ask me something like that? Of course I was going to keep it? I didn't and still don't believe in abortion. I had done this to myself but my baby was innocent and did not ask to be made. This was the righteous thing in my heart.

A child is a precious gift from God. How dare you both for even asking! I screamed at them both!

I don't know what he was thinking at the time but I just knew he was the answer to the way I was living all my life. Maybe he was going to get me my own apartment and my own car? Help me with raising this child? Or so I thought. Come to find out as the months passed one day I asked him what did he do for a living? Because he had always had all this money. I mean he was always throwing block parties and people crowding over there? Why was he so popular and praised? This man would always check his heart after sex with me with his stethoscope so I thought he was a doctor? He finally told me.

He was running one of the biggest fraud rings in Ohio. He was making fake checks and most of the people that would visit, mainly women, were working with him. I was devastated. Seventeen and pregnant. WTFlip! All my hopes just went down the toilet. Little did I know this man was under investigation as we spoke. What would I do if I had to raise this child on my own? I was screwed and losing it. Again. So I just said forget it he was going to be mines I don't care I had been through worse right?. By my sixth month of pregnancy I started noticing more and more women going over but not leaving at night. This was not just his girlfriend any more. But his girlfriend's niece and the girl from around the corner. One of them was visting from Columbus, Ohio and come to find out she was related to my aunt's husband, she was his sister and this was very awkward and created quite a stir! He was screwing everybody!

Soon I had given birth to my first little girl. She was 9 pds and 7 ounces. I was happy about my baby but devastated about my stomach. I had to have a C- Section due to my being extremely tiny in the pelvis and she was huge! I had went from 98 pds myself to 172 pds during my pregnancy. From a size zero to a size hippo lol. So after she was born I had a lot of extra stomach fat and had tried all the stomach creams to get rid of it. I was very sick because I had caught an infection during this procedure and the staples were awful. I was in a lot of pain. But I was just amazed that I was a mom. I loved my daughter's dad but I was always hurt by the things he would do. He even had sex with my close friend but this came later. I just went nuts!!! I had busted his window, egged his car, and often he had to call the police on me. But I had not known how desperate he had become because my anger was becoming rages of jealousy and on one occasion I was planning to kill him because of what he had done to me I slept under his porch just waiting for him to come outside and read his morning paper as he would usually do with only his robe on around five or six in the morning.

But this morning he did not appear because he was busy entertaining one of his girls. So I crawled back from under his porch and went home with dirt all over my clothing. My grandmother was just as embarrassed and tired of my silliness with this man!! They had said I had to move out and go back to live with my mother. This one time was because I would literally begin fighting my oldest daughter's dad. He was the first and the last man to ever give me a black eye. He did supply for her the necessary things and a little more but this was not what we really needed and he knew it. I think he was just more concerned with his case, the money, and women. Let's not leave me out, I was stabbing the porch, furious because I had to make a dang appointment to go see my daughter's dad and I hated the environment we were living in because there was constant fighting and arguing. The pressure was weighing in on me and family habits were rubbing off.

I even noticed my daughter beginning to develop a shaking habit and being very frightened because of all the violence. Not only was I jealous I felt I should not have had to do this and I had his baby. But I didn't leave yet! There was nowhere for me to go. Now I had a little girl. I had a little money and was just spending all of it on her and clothes and jewelry for her! She was spoiled. I also had been just giving money away to family and paying bills and buying groceries for everyone and they said I could stay. I had put some money away for my baby but when her dad had gotten down to his last move I had withdrawn her money and had given it to him to try and help, that was dumb. But I began to have a feeling of regret and more rage. Sometimes when we would argue I would put my daughter on his porch and walk off as if I didn't want her only to end up running right back to get her. Because I didn't want to be my mother but I was in many ways trying to get him to stop hurting me. No I did not leave her alone on a porch with no one home because he was there. But I still never should have even had the thought. Looking back no wonder I was an embarrassment even now my heart aches when I think about who I used to be when I would argue with this man. All my own thoughts of pain and resentment that I had. But I could never just walk away. I HAD TO GET MY BABY! BUT I WILL NEVER FORGET THE DAY I REALLY LOST MY CHILD FOR TWO MONTHS AND BECAUSE OF THIS I HAD the HARDDEST TIME FORGIVING HIM, because this time WE NEEDED HIM MORE THAN ANYTHING. But you will read this in a brief moment.

I was so gullible I didn't know what I was doing or what the real world was like. I was always creating drama out in the open with our business in the neighborhood I had stopped caring about him or the people what about our baby? He even had to put out a restraining order against me. I was just that fed up and pissed. I didn't want my daughter to end up without her dad and coming last to any woman so I was trying to force it. My grandmother said I had to leave. What will I do alone?

You see how I'm being used and even you used me and I still don't come first? I had lost my mind and began to be on these power trips more and more. I grew tired of always coming last in anyone's heart. One night I was at my mother's and she and I had gotten into an argument and I left with my baby to the pay phone and called him. Well I told him that our daughter and I needed come stay the night. He told me to call him back. I became furious because I come to you for you to take at least your daughter in and you tell me to call you back? I began walking up to his house with my baby in a stroller wrapped up in a lot of thick blankets and my comforter on top of her. Since my grandmother's house was on the same street I tried there first but no one was there.

So I went around the corner where this old salon used to be and sat there for a while with her.

This just made me even angrier. So I walked my daughter to his house and knocked on the back door. I heard loud music and another woman which one I didn't know was there nor did I care. He finally came to the door and I noticed he was naked and he looked through the curtain and walked away as if I was not even there. Before I knew it I was banging on the glass of the back door and had broken the window. I saw this woman begin to panic and she also was naked and said what the hell is going on?

It was his girlfriend. I didn't care, my only concern was your child needs to spend the night until I clear my head and figure out what I'm going to do and you will not forsake our daughter for your little girlfriend by allowing her to sleep outdoors with me.

Then I turned grabbed her and sat her down wrapped in the blanket. I walked away and took a walk until I decided to just return and go get her and maybe my grandmother was home. By the time I got to the corner I saw police cruisers and news crews and my mom noticed me she had made her way up there and my grandmother and family was there.

This man had told these people that some strange young girl had left a baby on his porch and he does not know whose child it was…What did he say? Just like my dad and my life now I have to see my child go through this?

Then I was advised by family to admit myself into a mental institution because I almost lost all reality. I went into this facility and stayed the evening there but barely slept because my fear was me becoming my mom and my daughter growing up like me. The next day they almost didn't even let me out of there, the therapist said he wanted to make sure I was completely calm before allowing me to leave once he had found out what happened but he allowed my departure. I flew up to children services and immediately begged for my child. They had put her into the system for two months and this nearly killed me. I nearly just drank myself away and my oldest aunt Nicole took custody in which made me feel better because I will get to see her regularly and make sure she has all she needs.

Well even that came with a price of 150 a month that even children services knew nothing about but since my aunt had admitted to them I purchased all her clothing, still provide shoes, pampers, and money even would babysit her while she's working they just went on ahead and gave me back my child. They truly had no case against me for I was a righteous mother who had just made a bad choice of regret. I'm still having trouble with that memory.

I do appreciate my aunt at least doing that much even though they took money from my mom and there are a bunch of lies and abuse toward my mom and I that at least was an act of righteousness.

I had no idea the FBI was always around watching everything and soon he was going to jail. He did not have the time because he was running out of time. I was selfish but had every right to be! I was fed up with it all!

One day I walked in on them and he was sitting there with the men in black! He was being arrested it was over. So I had gotten my own place in the projects. That didn't last long. Remember I told you about him sleeping with my close friend. Well I accused her falsely because it wasn't her.

It was the other girl who used to hang out with us. And this girl lived around the corner from me in the projects and had two kids already. I was going over her house after I moved in my apartment and it all came out after my daughter's dad had gotten locked up.

Chapter Sixteen

Betrayal

I WAS GOING OVER THERE crying about how scared I was to do it alone raising my baby and asking her how could our friend do this to me? How could she betray me? Whenever this girl wanted to hang out or even when I needed someone to talk to I would hang out with her but guess what? It was her! She was my betrayer. She had slept with my daughter's dad. And in my eyes he was a slimy bastard. How could he? I couldn't trust anyone. I wanted to fight her but was threatened by a girl who was known for fighting if I fought her. I was not prepared for that. And had become so irritated I left my apartment. I had never been jumped. I came back to my apartment and it was broken into. They had taken all my daughter's things. I retaliated towards my oldest daughter's dad in the worst way.

I was hanging out with a friend like relative who was dating this strange and unusual guy when I was introduced to a young man who was actually interested in my little cousin but once he found out her age he decided he wanted to talk to me. I was not interested because I do not consider myself to be second choice but also my other cousin was very interested in this guy. His name was Darion, only thing is he was not the least bit interested in her.

We hung out the rest of the night but upon us going to this man's house to play a game of cards I realized once we pulled up that this house was my daughter's sister's home or so I thought because I remember driving in the car with my child's dad to this very same house. So I left well enough alone that time. I didn't go back to my apartment. I went back to live with my grandmother but everyone in my family was talking bad of me and saying she can't stay here for free.

All my little money had run out so I was not anything but a burden any more. I went to stay with my mother who I had found out was dabbling with crack cocaine as well with her still boyfriend. Actually all my aunts and uncles except for one was messing with it. I knew this because the streets talk.

And though I was not in them often the guys who were selling it always knew who my family members were and what they did. Plus my mother's dude would always talk to my mom bout certain argument's they would have when they were hanging out with her siblings and their boyfriends and mutual friends and I would be ease dropping and heard a lot of what they were really doing.

So in my spare time in which I had a lot of I was still hanging out. I went over to this family friend's house and there was the guy again who she kept trying to hook me up with. We hung out again and this time he had given me a ride home at the end of the evening. We talked in his car for a while and I told him the reasons why I couldn't mess around with him like that. He and I realized that my daughter's dad was his sister's dad also. They had the same sister. This house that my child's dad and I had went to was not her sister's home but was the home of the mother of this man I was sitting with in the car. My daughter's step brother!

My child and this man were step brother and sister because my daughter's dad had never gotten a divorce! Ohh my daughter's dad made me sick! Come to find out this man had told me that my daughter's dad had also tried to talk to his children's mother as in a sexual interest so this angered us both! But still I asked him how he felt about my cousin, because she had a big crush on him but she also had a crush on the guy next door to her cousin who kept trying to hook us up. This girl was a big liar and good at being this way. I would always wonder how someone could be good a being bad? But hey look at me? I thought I was the coldest when it came down to doing wrong things but ended up looking the dumbest. Because this was never who I truly was in the first place. Darion explained to me that he feels that she was a cool person but he was not interested in a girl like her. But that his brother he would try to hook up with her because his brother was more of the good guy lol.

I was already extremely heated angry about everything I had just found out about my daughter's dad on top of everything else he had already done, so I just said you know what? I would love to go home with you. Whoa! Was I really going to do this? I remember asking myself. Elisheva you're not a bad girl. You don't need to do this I thought. Then the adversary came and whispered in my ear…Remember what your own little girl's dad did to you who you used to adore. He had your heart and spit on it. This man and I had driven to his home and I didn't back out.

Chapter Seventeen

Deception

I WENT IN AND WE sat on the black couch. He leaned in and kissed me and boy was it good. This again was the devil's temptation and me reacting out of hatred, revenge, and pain. Not knowing that this was one of many of the evil tools the enemy uses to brainwash you into believing doing wrong will make you feel better. See he was very handsome and a lot of women were after him. But I was such a lil nerd for real I never knew how popular this guy was. I just thought about the hurt I had to endure from a broken heart so I kissed him back.

Then I felt his hands moving slowly up and down my legs. Clothes began to come off and I whispered in his ear "Are you sure you want to do this"? He looked at me and asked. Are you sure? Next thing I knew I said yes.

And I received him into my body. I was a mess. I regret this because for a few moments of pleasure I sold out. At the time all I could think about was how it felt good both to get back at my child's dad and how this man touched me. Thing is young ladies he didn't give two cents care about me either. Because that's all I was, just something to do for the moment. DO NOT REACT OFF OF YOUR EMOTIONS I KNOW NOW FROM EXPERIENCE!

I had given in too easy but just didn't realize it yet. That's why it's better to wait on GOD to bring you a husband instead of searching on your own. We made love and I actually made love to him. The reason why I say this is because not often did I actually give real sexual emotion to a man I engaged in sex with except for my old heart. I held back a lot because I believe every man is not supposed to know how you are in the bed unless you're going to love and be with him. Now I realize you just wait on GOD to direct your paths period because, look how many lessons I had to learn and heart breaks I endured just to realize what true love is. Every day I am still fighting to find my way to feel GOD'S love all over me and every new experience never gets old. I have been waiting and what a beautiful feeling not to think of myself as a jezebel anymore or just someone's candy girl. Because I know JESUS THY GOD LOVES ME. He never walks out on me and gives me another day to start again, fight again, love again, live again in him. But during my past this was the Big PAYBACK!!! So I really gave this man me but for just that night only.

He dropped me off after and I did not call him. But surprisingly he popped up over my grandmother's one day and we kept it up for a while but it didn't last long because I did not know love and don't think I ever did. I was just acting out of pain and began just playing the game but doing a horrible job of it. I never knew what I wanted and often had to wonder if I've ever really wanted him or just the control at the time? See I had become highly sexual, very flirtatious, rude, and self- centered. That answer to this day is no. Not by a human man. I let him use me just like I had let all the others who walked in and out of my life.

I got a job at Macy's and hated it but it was a job. My boss lived directly around the corner from me. She would even give me a ride to work. But my mom said that she was not keeping any kids, and that I was her mother and I was going to have to stop working cause she had a man and had things to do. This was said in front of my boss and my boss just looked at me. She tried to speak up for me but my mom said I said what I said this is my daughter.

And that was that. See my boss had offered to give me rides to work because she stayed right around the corner and she knew the things that were going on with me once she began to give me rides we got a little close. I admired her because she too was a single mother her daughter was grown but she told me how she worked hard and fought to keep her child and get the position she had there at Macy's she was the boss! I loved her and she was just so amazing to me. But due to the circumstances I had lost out on a job. Which I didn't understand again.

I started hanging back over my grandmother's and getting drunk all of the time. My mom was no longer just the black sheep of the family. I was slowly moving into her position. As long as I had some money I was cool but when I would become drunk and broke I was just young, dumb, and a failure in my mind. Just out there wasting my life and laying up with men who said they loved me after they would get me drunk. I'm not saying that I was not loved by my family at all but I am saying that no one really tried to help me as much as they could have. See in my family it's a little like as long as it's not my kid I don't care or if you have money and all the nice fancy things and dress nice you're the one who's taken to by everyone. But if you were the poorest you were nothing more than just there.

I didn't have any idea what love really was. I lost my identity. I didn't know who I was anymore. I stayed drunk and almost all of the time ended up into arguments with my aunts and uncles. One night my uncle came home high on crack cocaine and liquor and asked me to make him something to eat because he was hungry. So I went into the kitchen and made him some food.

Outta nowhere he just started calling me b#tches and saying how I was a no body and a dropout who had nothing and got pregnant. I got angry and we began to argue. He said B#tch come outside and I'm going to beat your ass! I was completely sick of how people treated me and so I went knowing I could not beat this man. He punched me in my mouth and I cracked a beer bottle and cut him with it on his arm. Thank you JESUS he ended up alright. Thank you JESUS I never had to do any real time.

We both ended up in jail and I knew then I had enough. Charges were dropped and we both got out of jail. Unfortunately for me I also got a domestic violence charge which kept me from getting a job as a STNA anywhere. I didn't realize that the choices you make in life even in self-defense can lead you into a life of doors closing that could have at least been a way to get myself together until later on when I tried to apply for these jobs. I had lost respect for them and my mother.

Chapter Eighteen

Lost

ONE NIGHT ONE OF MY aunts were going to fight me
because of my mouth and they too had said some pretty
nasty things about me, comparing me to my mother and I had to
get out again with my baby at my grandmothers. My mother and
brother jumped in the middle of my aunt and I and I had to stroll
my baby up the street with them in the middle of the night. But
I always went back to stay there and kick it. That was all I knew
anymore. My aunt was then dating a guy that I had found out
was my distant cousin on my dad's side of the family. He knew a
lot of people and used to box and father had become the council
man. But he too was a little black sheep because he had a drinking
problem. One day while walking to the store with him he was
stopped by a man in a Youngstown City Gas Co. truck.

This was his friend from way back. This man his name was Rico.
He said hello to me and asked my cousin who I was. My daughter
was three at the time. My cousin said oh her man that's my little
cousin and my girlfriend's niece which sounded odd but he didn't

care. We became cool and I began going to the east side over to his house. See he seemed cool but he too had a girlfriend and was trying to sneak around with me and date me. I was on the Depo shot which is supposed to prevent you from getting pregnant but I did. Pregnant again by this man Rico with the red corvette and in the motorcycle gang. I was seeing the both of them at the same time.

He was prepared to give me the money to abort the baby but I just didn't have the guts because I still did not believe in them. I found out he was abusive to his girlfriend and was a little racist. I knew this because I had begun seeing this man who said he was going to try to get me to finish school and into the military. See he was a recruiter and he was for the U.S. Army. I called myself taking the ASVAB test. Yes I failed in this with no GED but gained this recruiters interest.

But he began to like me and started coming around and taking me out to dinner. He was white and this was a problem for the man I was pregnant by. But this recruiter was married and getting a divorce from his wife. Due to both parties being unfaithful before I even entered into the situation. We began sleeping together after because it started at first as just favors of another sexual interest. He would pay me for sexual favors and I was just looking at it as business. We were both two people who were very lonely but once we both realized I couldn't get in the military he kind of took advantage of the whole damsel in distress thing. I was very vulnerable but not innocent. I was committing adultery. I was a home wrecker in my eyes but a mother trying to feed her daughter also because I was living off of the gov't and I was not happy so I started dancing for money and stripping. But not long due to the fact I ended up having personal clientele and was soon tricking and didn't even know that was the title for what I was doing. I had male friends with their own car lots and optical businesses. I was doing this for no less than $150.00 a pop and had no feelings for them. I hated my life. I had become a cheap harlot thinking that I was doing what I had to do for my children. Staying drunk to get through my reality and this was no good. And I was doing what I had to but in the wrong ways. I always had to drown myself in alcohol to make the arrangement go quicker.

But loved my daughter. I would do almost anything to keep her clothed and fed until I can figure out where she and I will officially end up although we had shelter I didn't trust it. I had kept trying the stripping a few times. I think I was the worst stripper ever. I thank You JESUS it's over. But mainly personal private business. Staying drunk, drunk, drunk, and eventually trying to smoke weed in which I could never handle. I felt like a withering flower. Or a tree through the autumn days. As the seasons change the leaves turn color and fall until eventually all of the leaves have gone and the tree is bare. The beauty of this process is when it begins to bloom again. This was me starting over and dying over. Repetitiously never looking at the beauty GOD had given or even allowing the blooming process. I had lost my mind a minute.

Chapter Nineteen

Adultery, & the False Marriage

B Y THIS TIME I JUST didn't care about men or myself. All I cared for was my daughter because I knew that I was just something for them to have sex with, a play thing, but if I was going to do this I was going to get something out of it. This had become what I thought was living.

We started out by me going to Burger King taking the test, to him saying it's not looking too good for me to join. I would first have to get a GED, then give temporary custody of my daughter to someone to be in boot camp for 6 months but I didn't have anyone all I had was a roof over my head from place to place and laying on my back for money to feed my daughter.

So we started flirting and he said he liked me. We became messing around but first he was paying for oral sex. I always made sure I was drunk whenever I pulled any tricks. But the man I got pregnant by was getting his information on me from someone and had it in his mind I set him up to become pregnant by him.

LMAO, I didn't know what I was looking for but it darn sure was not another baby. Especially by him. Although I still had a looking for love issue I knew he was not the one. He started ignoring me saying I was crazy. And I stopped tricking around and it was the white man who was by my side every single step of my pregnancy. He would say he loved me and didn't care if my child wasn't his baby. But everyone always laughed at him and I calling us the odd couple because I was black he was white.

He was country because he was from Texas and I was from the ghetto. I was tall and he was extremely short. Funny thing is no matter how much they laughed at him he still came around for me and my baby. And if they needed anything from him he would always reach in his pocket to give them. These same friends and family of mines that would laugh at my ole boot camp and I.

So he confessed he loved me but I told him I did not feel the same. I cared for him but I don't think I loved anyone anymore except my baby. He proposed to me and I was pressured into it by my family and this man. They said I would be stupid not to and he knew I had nothing or no one. It was my vulnerleablility he used to pry on. I knowing this thought I was using it to my advantage but instead I was being trapped into an unfaithful oath and didn't even know it. Because I had not done anything with my life and everyone had so many expectations for me when becoming an adult, I wanted to please my family. Boot camp proposed right in front of my family where he knew I did not want to embarrass him. My family kept pulling me to the side trying to convince me he would be the one. My grandmother and mother and aunts and uncles, cousins and all just because of what he had and that was money to give away. But this was not my dream marriage, I wanted to love my husband, honor and obey. Long to be laying next to him and grow old with him and go before GOD in truth. This was not the truth. The tears I cried the day of my marriage at city hall were not happy tears. I never understood how a man can knowingly push someone into being with them when he knew the woman did not love him? Why would you want that? I guess his spirit rubbed off on me because I ended up with this same spirit when I left 8 months later. But when I had my daughter he was right there. That's right I had another girl, 8 pds and 4 ounces. and she was beautiful.

I could never say boot camp was a bad guy. Just that after his 3 marriages before me and all my bad events not to mention the way we met during one of my many times of prostitution was just not where I wanted to be. I walked away willing to return to the ghetto than to continue to live a lie of unhappiness, deception, adultery, confusion, and laying through the night in the arms of a man that I could never soulfully connect to in giving myself 100%. I was just there, happier when he was at work or when I would travel home to see my family. I had love for him but I could never fall in love with him. This man used to pay me for sexual favors, I could never view him and I as serious.

I sometimes think he may too have been just afraid to be alone. I think the time he and I met was the time when I began to have a heart of stone. I felt as if I had lost everything already and now, I had lost my dignity as well as my identity. Who can love such a woman? Who can really see through this skin and find out what's deep inside? A heart that has a fire kindling of a passion for freedom and somehow got mangled in her own web? No this was not a kind feeling any longer. As cunning as the sign of my nature I had now a venom that matched my name. I never knew just how much poison a scorpion could inject but I would soon find out.

I injected myself with my own poison at times crippling myself away from freedom. Wanting CHRIST but fleeing from him every time because I couldn't understand being alone. I forgot what I had saw on the television that night at the hospital as a child, and how GOD himself came down on earth in the flesh to save my life and yours, and all I had to do was accept him into my heart and forgive. But the word forgive was like a sour taste flowing from my lips and I could not even stomach the thought. My mind kept going over my mom, my dad, my kids, and their dad's. I had become wife number four to an unwanted marriage and my heart was bitter sweet. I wanted my children's dad's to love, want, and at least come and see them. Especially my second daughter's dad at this time.

But her dad only came to see her a few times. He had started saying that she was not his. Strangely he only said this when her skin started turning from light to dark. But I couldn't understand why he was the one upset because see, his father was a very dark skinned Hispanic and his mother was a very dark skinned African American woman so she didn't get it from me. None the less I loved her for she was my child, a part of me. I didn't care what color she was, she was a beautiful dark brown gift from GOD with beautiful dark silky curly hair. How could he say such a thing? He stopped wanting to care for her after a while. I tried giving him the benefit of the doubt and not taking him to child support but he was still just giving me 40 or 50 bucks for her and this was not enough after all he has a job for the city. This was not much money and I couldn't deal with that mess. So I finally went in to child support on him. He wouldn't even see her. To be honest I used to get angry because I can't even in the now list any one of their dads as an emergency contact for their schools or hospital visits. But again Through It All JESUS Kept Me Strong! I DIDN'T NEED THEM THEN AND DON'T NEED THEM NOW. THEY HAVE A FATHER AND HIS NAME IS JESUS!

Also I was angry that he kept denying her to his girlfriend I'm not going to lie yes that's another reason. Because my father had done that to me and my mother and I hated that. So this ticked him off and the fight was on. To this day we no longer speak he just pays his child support and when my daughter asks how come my dad does not write me or come to see me or want me. I don't know how to respond so I just tell her baby I love you and I'm here and don't worry about it. She can't even call him.

I will never and have never ever loved him and that's the truth but you don't treat your own kid that way because she has done nothing but been born into this world which you helped to give life and for this foul treatment of her you will have to answer to GOD.

But that's between him and GOD. At least he pays his child support but I only think it's because he does not want to lose his license for if this happens that will interfere with his twenty something years of being with the co. I couldn't stand them. I'm still working on it. Forgiveness is better now. I feel free, I am free.

I soon left. See the man in the military had grew tired of hearing me talk about how I wanted to leave Youngstown and move somewhere quiet, have my own home, and new way of living. My grandmother's illness had gotten worse and she had passed. I had my own place by that time again but no furniture and was still not working. He had officially divorced and I met his kids who lived with their mom except for his oldest.

She was in Texas and I had not met her yet but I loved those little girls. They were sweet little girls and so adorable! I did not see race as the issue. My problem was love.He told me he was going to be re-stationed and that he wanted me to come with. I told him no at first cause I wasn't really sure but he promised I would love it. I would not have to deal with the people who ever hurt me anymore.

I thought about it and was afraid but I took my daughters and left. We ended up in a small town that was just getting over the prejudice hump and we had the nerve to be an interracial couple. The house was nice. For the first time I had a kitchen I had fallen in love with five bedrooms and two bathrooms. I was in love with the house but still not with the man who was renting it.

So I lost a lot of interest in having sex with him and began sleeping on the couch heck I even had stopped wanting men.

I actually began to become curious about women. And attracted to them. I had completely had no idea of just how lost I was anymore.

Men no longer satisfied me I even began to wonder had they truly ever satisfied me? Who was I? I ended up messing around with a girl. But the guilt after wards was horrible. I felt as if I had shamed God and was unworthy of his love. First of all so many people had convinced me that GOD hated Gay people but that's not true!! He hates the sin of what we as his creation are doing not the person. But it is not something he approves of! And not only that I had spent my life fornicating, got married and still didn't understand what I was doing, but I did know it was wrong! We all have a conscious.

See what I never realized was whenever you get that feeling of guilt in doing anything you are doing in life that you know is not right....rather you go to church or not that is GOD'S spirit in and all around you allowing you to feel that that right there should help you in choosing not to do some of the things you do. But at the time I was highly ignorant of GOD'S love, grace, and mercy. How could I not love this man I married? Right when I need to love the most.

Chapter Twenty

The Confusion

WHEN SOMEONE FINALLY HAD LOVED me but I could not give any to him. When you just marry out of convenience it's never love. Stability or just to be married or even allowing someone to make you do things you don't want to is NEVER right! I always ended up creating more problems for myself because I always tried pleasing people instead of allowing GOD to help me find what He wanted for me. I kept fighting GOD and remained being led by people who were lost themselves. I didn't even know that being gay was a part of having spiritual loss and sexual entities in and around you. But still I do not regret leaving because I felt my oath to GOD in marriage was a lie. Money and stability. Was it worth my soul?

I was still staying drunk and had become spoiled. Everyone at home had heard how I had left with this white man and soon I began getting talked about and laughed at pretty bad. This always bothered me but I was so dumb I didn't realize that I didn't have to worry about them. GOD had brought me to a place where none of them mattered but by this time my heart was hardened and blinded. This did not last long. I left and went back home where really there was no home. I had ruined my own sanctuary. And returned to hell. This man kept trying to get me to come back but I wouldn't and by the time I wanted to. His heart too had become hardened. I ended up seeing my very first love later but he had walked in with some girl. We were over and old mutual friend's house.

And he didn't know I was there. He was shocked to see me and I was hurt to see him again. And with some girl. All my anger came back like you never came back. You didn't want me the one who told you to go in the first place but you just look past me every time. So my anger took over me and there was this fine guy there. Trying to get with me and this man said ride to the store with me. I said I was waiting on my old friend to come back but he said what are you worried over him for? Didn't you see him with his girl? What? His girl? Sure I'll ride with you and anywhere else you want to go. It didn't take much for me to do something stupid.

Chapter Twenty One

Making It Worse...

I SLEPT WITH HIM. AND when I got back there was my old flame just sitting there playing cards and looking at me. I didn't know he was really coming back. I figured he was just like the rest and I had grown tired.

But he got his vengeance. He slept with a family friend. But I had it coming to me. And though I could not become jealous I was broken hearted. She and I fought. Thing is even as angry as I was I just couldn't hit her but before I knew it she hit me. The reason I could not hit her is because she was practically in my eyes still like a little cousin and I just didn't see her as my enemy for real no matter how much I was speaking in anger about her or him. He still had my heart and she still had my heart. To this day I love them both strangely.

I ended up just leaving and going to Cincinnati to try to go to school. I finally thought I had come to some sort of agreement with my mother and had given her temporary custody and put her name up over my lease in the apartment I had moved into. But she ended. Right back with the guy I tried to keep her from. He was in my home.

I would call home and people in my family as well as my landlord told me to come get my kids. Even Ms. Donna my landlord shocked me because she said baby I am so proud of you for joining the Cincinnati Job Corps facility and I never thought I would ever tell anyone trying to pursue their education this but you come get these kids! I'm going to have to evict you but if you all move out I'll just have to put all of the fines towards your credit.

And my credit was already bad. I got home and Ms. Donna met me in my old apartment and I walked in in total shock. It was destroyed. And I was hurt. My uncle showed me to the motel where my mom had my kids living and they were looking pretty rough, hair, matted, high waters, and bummy shirts, shoes dirty and completely just unbearable, I was MAD!

I hated to have to leave but if I didn't I would be kicked out of the program and so my mom kept the girls. She soon left and her and the girls came to Cincinnati and my brother. They had to stay in a shelter. But soon my mom got her own place and was on section 8.

I would leave campus every day and see about my kids and they had clothes because I made sure of that and my mom had begun to straighten up. But we were still at each other's throat and I had no respect for her. She was still always kicking me out and so I had gotten a job with the post office but Job corps said I had to quit because I was not a graduate yet.

So either quit or get kicked out of the program. I should've just left Job Corps because I was kicked out anyways. I had an affair going on with one of the Staff and he was a mess. He was messing with alot of us there come to find out. LOl but of course this was the story of my life. I ended up being called to a meeting but took alot of the blame for the scandal. So no more Job Corps. I ended up meeting a man and tricking with him another sugar daddy. I had a job but money was never enough and I began singing with a Rap group that never made it or if they did they damn sure was not going to give a dime of anything to me. I was soon contacted by my now grown sister who had just gotten 25,000 and I didn't know at the time. She asked me if she can come stay with me and I said yes but when she came she was extremely jealous of me.

She hated me ever since she was a small girl and every time I would bring her to the studio she would deliberately start arguments with me and I was soon kicked out from the group. I hated my family and soon left and went to Atlanta to stay with a cousin. Well my cousin and I fell out and I was once again place to place. So I was again using my body to get by. This is when I met a man named Dave. He was white from the mid-west just like me and he was looking to hang out. I had on a skirt which showed my legs and he was the first guy who I had met with a leg fettish. I had no money and no one to keep my kids while looking for a job. Dave invited me out to dinner and we talked and came to an arrangement. I was no longer broke. I was making sure my kids were taken care of but only stayed there for a few months. Dave and I travelled with me and my kids back to Ohio. He left and went to Chicago. I picked up my mom who was just beginning to get sick but we just didn't know it yet.

Dave wired me money to go to Cincinnati to pick up my old music and that's when all hell broke loose again. The incident with the music group I was with took place and then Dave wired me money to get back to Atlanta but once I arrived at the Condo it was empty and had nowhere to go. When I called and asked why he said it was because he got fired from his job as an engineer and just couldn't handle coming back to Georgia. I had two kids and his were grown.

Later I went back to stay with relatives but things went wrong again. So we left and found another relative who was there and she had gotten me a job at Best Car Was & Lube. I didn't even know my employer was well known in the industry of music.

Because things went so badly I left Atlanta and never did get to sing for my employer Mr. Simone at Best Car Wash and Lube. See he had bought the place but surprisingly to me he was famous for a hot track by Boys to Men.

But he didn't like being approached by people with talent trying to get a record deal or anything like that and now I know why. My mom had come with me there to Atlanta but again remember she was very sick. She had a heart condition. So did her mother who had passed and her sister who passed shortly after her mom. I was freaked out and we had to come back to Ohio because we were kicked out of where we were staying. So I lived with the only person who would take us in when we arrived. Not family but my friend Elicia from back in school. She was living in the projects and advised me to get one. It had been five years I was gone away from Youngstown and had returned the same way I had left.

With nothing no GED, no job, no home, and no money. I blamed my mother for everything. But I was the one who had never had the heart to leave my family. This was all my fault. Choices I made. But it always felt good to point the finger at someone else. Even though some of the reasons life for me was hell it was time for me to grow up but I never had.

Chapter Twenty Two

Still Searching

MY MOM EVENTUALLY GOT INTO an argument with my friend and was quite disrespectful, so this put a damper in my friend's and I relationship. She put us out but waited until my apartment was ready to do so. It was a trip. One day we found after mom had been in the emergency room that she had to have emergency open heart surgery. I was afraid I was going to lose her and I went outside to the front to smoke. Even so I can't say I would have dealt with it either but I just should not have done it in that manner. But who knows because I myself had done shady things in my life.

I met a young man there. His name was Darnell. Seemed like every time I needed time to heal the devil just kept em coming and I kept falling for it. And he said he was picking up his mother. He was not my type, had big lips, tall, heavy set, and goofy. I told him I would call him and I did after two weeks. My mom had gotten out of the hospital and I was trying to take care of her.

But when she got well enough she would leave and go visit ex friends that were not good for her. You all know who that meant and so the arguing and fighting with us began again and I would sometimes put her out of my house.

I did not want this man with my mother or around my children. One night I called the young man I had met at the hospital when I had gotten upset I always thought that either running to a man or a drink was going to ease my pain, he and I ended up hanging out. He was so sweet and when I needed something he was there.

I moved out of the projects, I never stayed in any project in Youngstown for more than six months surprisingly to me even though I was always not blessed with a good education or a lot of money. But I got a house on the south side and this man got my water turned on and bought my kids food I mean filled that fridge up! He wasn't having that non sense as long as he was around. Only problem is he was sleeping with his baby mamma, a couple girls around the way, and one of my closest family friends step sister's cousin. I know this because I caught him with her one night.

So I did the unthinkable and met up with her and purposely slept with her. I knew she was a lesbian because I used to go through his phone and read all of the hurtful messages from different females. So I made sure I made a laughing stock of him in front of his boys but who really ended up the laughing stock?

It was me. I had lost the trust of his mom and mines and also embarrassed myself by not maintaining the role of a woman who could have just walked away but by that time I felt like I had went through too much with him. ISAIAH CH 3 VERSE 16-24. I had to learn this lesson up until the age I am now 32. But not then.

See soon after he and I met I had found out that his daughter's mom had tragically died in an accident, but everyone else had said he was the one who did it! Do you know what it's like to be in love with someone who people are calling a murderer? And seeing a man cry when you try to end it but he says he needs you and you're the only one who believes him. That he doesn't know what to do? And people are looking at you like you're the wrong one? Well I do.

Chapter Twenty Three

Choices

I GUESS THE REASON I stayed was because I knew what it was like to have people laugh at you or not want to deal with you, not knowing anything about me or what was wrong with my life or why I did the things I did. I believed that everyone needs somebody and I was not designed to turn people away or judge people GOD had that right and I knew what it was like to be crapped on like the scum of the earth. So I stayed even though I grew many enemies due to this. Every time I looked up I was being scorned, mocked, ridiculed and neglected because of this. But still I could not walk away from him seeing the tears in his eyes. It's always best to let GOD handle it!

See this man had been a pill popper before I met him but I believe it had gotten worse when all this happened in his life. He popped so many pills his mouth began to develop this white nasty substance in the corners of his lips. I sometimes thought he would end up overdosing.

But I could not deal with the cheating and refused to so I did start judging after that but I was digging my own punishment because GOD was watching and waiting for me to wake up from my own nightmare I kept creating! Study showing me that it's not a man I need or my mother's love or the approval of people, I NEEDED HIM!!!

After that he and I separated and I began seeing an old friend in Atlanta I didn't mention who eventually took me to Myrtle Beach South Carolina. I was angered that this man was afraid of the beach water but had come there for a vacation.

So I would take walks when the sun was setting above the water and just think of my life. I would think of how I went from wanting to be a marine biologist to having two kids whose fathers' were not there? I remembered how I would always be so hard on my mom and say that I would never be like her. But I was.... So something said step your feet into the water and sit down as the waves move over your body and talk to GOD. Ask for his forgiveness and some sense of direction in your life. I cried a lot at that spot on the beach away from my friend. But I would not tell him.

The trip was over and I had come home. I called my other old flame Dave and he invited me to visit Las Vegas! I was not going to pass this up cause I always wanted to see Vegas at night. So he flew me to Chicago to see him where he lived and from there we flew to Vegas.

Boy my first plane ride was scary but I thought we were going to have to enjoy ourselves, only thing is he stayed at the black jack table and I was afraid to go anywhere alone. And the MGM was nice but had no one to go anywhere with so I stayed in the room a lot. I was unhappy. See through all the shopping and all the dinners and even the Hoover Dam I still felt empty, this was not fun because there was no love. I began to realize that it was always just these men that I would choose and become their eye candy and sex toy. I went home. I was still missing something?

Chapter Twenty Four

Always Sky

WELL MY DAUGHTER'S HAD A special after school
and I had come to get them. But there I saw a very old
friend. It was my Sky from high school! He was in the cafeteria
serving food to the kids with his aunt.

We hugged when he had gotten a break and exchanged numbers.
There were rumors that he was gay and I didn't want to just come
out and ask him that. But I had always liked him and wanted to
be his girl in school now was my chance I had to say something.

He ended up coming over very often for coffee and we would just
talk for hours and he introduced me to the gospel artist Detrick
Haddon. I had never heard music to the Lord this way and my
friend Mr. Amazing, Mr. Wonderful had never judged me or
called me weird for listening to my ENYA or ENIGMA or Native
American, African, Soca, Ragae, or Lite Rock. He even said he
liked some of the tracks on the cd Pure Moods! I could be myself
I didn't have to pretend anymore! Well, all I can say is we had

gotten a little too close and we were intimate but not just as lovers but as intimate friends.

He always kept me in prayer even though we knew we seriously had to change our lives individually and put GOD first! But just the fact that someone finally had come along and I could be me was awesome. But most of all I started praying and was finding out that GOD loved me more than anyone could ever love me! Now I had my heart broken again by this man because he too had been lost. He couldn't quite figure out where he wanted to be.

He was having affairs that I could not judge because I myself had fallen short of God's glory for because i strayed away from who I was in my identity as well.

So I was wrong to say anything but I could not continue to put myself out there and always come last to anyone else. So we were off and on for a while. I refused to come second to anyone anymore. I was trying to change and it wasn't fair for me to pressure my one true male friend but it was also unfair for me to risk my heart again for the love I had for him! But to this day he is my best friend and my love as well as my first choice in command over my kids unless I become married!!

Chapter Twenty Five

Unfaithfulness

I MOVED FROM THAT HOUSE into an apartment and my ex and I were supposed to be getting back together but he had gotten locked up and was released to a drug rehabilitation facility for selling drugs and was now getting passes to leave. I would at times go pick him up but this one particular time he lied and said he was not being released.

But I ended up going anyways and caught him in the car with his kids' mother. Now I don't care if you have a baby's mother...you are supposed to do for your kids and be there for them. But when you lie about being with or around your kids mom you are not just lying to me your sleeping with her. You think you can just use me and go to her and all these other women you're wrong. He had also burned me too many times and I was just too damn angry to forget. When I say burned me I mean literally he had given me an STD. I was to take pills and had to get a shot because of this. So instead of learning from this I still went out and slept with three other men. THREE! Staying drunk in my misery and depression. No respect for myself. Listening to songs about being a bad A#$$ B%&#H! Listening to all the lies of satan in the music being sung by various artists to this day.

I had to endure embarrassment and shame that I loved someone who did not truly love me. So once again I hardened my heart and thought I was getting even. I was working at Citi Trends clothing store and ended up on a pay day late one night after work getting with an old flame Trevor who I purposely failed to mention because this story is way old of how he and I met. Now my daughter was 8 years old and I had don good for 8 years not laying down until all that anger had gotten the best of me. Because one night I guess I thought I was too dang safe, just because the man I ended up sleeping with was a guy I had been sleeping with eight years off and on and never got pregnant… well, I got pregnant. Not again NO NO NO!!!! These were the thoughts running through my mind.

This dude I had slept with had a girl and I had a guy I was trying to love even though it was not going to well. This was always the wrong way of meeting anyone because I kept choosing to be second to other women and for what?

Well I didn't know whose kid it was. Cause I was just giving up on myself doing anything to ease the pain! I was drinking the first 6 months of my pregnancy. Everyday!

I didn't want my baby this time. I had grown tired of doing the wrong things and choosing the right thing because of it. But after my 6th month I had stopped. But I was very ill a lot. At all my appointments they had said that the baby was always ok. But when I gave birth to Gabrielle she was not breathing. I was freaking out asking GOD please! Please don't take my baby I'm so sorry for saying I didn't want her please forgive me! Finally after about almost one a minute I heard a cry. That was the loudest and prettiest cry I had heard in my life! She was pale white and grey? It was weird but she had a head full of hair and gorgeous, 8 pds and 13.4 ounces! I said LORD I would have gotten rid of this beautiful gift? I'm sorry JESUS.

Chapter Twenty Six

Thankful

THANK YOU JESUS FOR SPARING my child and giving me a chance from my foolishness! After my 3 days were up of being in the hospital I could not leave with my baby because my baby was sick. She had caught an infection on the way out of the birth canal? I thought it was something I did. Did I have a disease I asked my doctor?

No he said I didn't do anything but she had caught an infection on the way out during her birth. I was devastated and was there every day during her seven day stay I even would sleep in the hospital waiting rooms. But soon they would give me private rooms to at least give her milk and be with her. See I had never really breast fed any of my other children but at that moment the doctors made me realize how a mother's milk is more healthier in a situation like this and that's when GOD made me realize even more the importance of life and my job as a mother.

I didn't care that again the father would not be by my side once I realized that it was my children not me who was most important. It didn't matter that I didn't have a lot, GOD assured me that he had all the power and I was going to stand up once again and I was not alone! It's like she knew when I was there, she would look so peacefully and smile!

They began making me go home to get some sleep at times and I did. But came back every day until finally I could take my baby home to her sisters and granny! I know it was only seven days but to me it felt like a lifetime because that feeling was the most guilt I have ever felt in my life. GOD showed me he was GOD and truly merciful, I had better get my act together!

Well soon after I couldn't figure out who was her dad so we took blood tests to find out who my child's father was. She was not my boyfriends...she was the other guys. But the boyfriend was the one buying her milk and pampers and in my corner. He was the one who would burp her after her feedings and hold her in his arms looking at how beautiful she was wondering why I did it? Why I couldn't wait and this little girl should have been his? I was a foolish girl and still was lost to my own ways of confusion.

He would never forgive me and now I had to deal with this one over here who was hiding yet again that he was my child's dad. She came last and again I had to watch as one of my kids came last to another woman again. I stayed there in that apartment until I moved to the north side. It was during this time that my mother and I had another argument and this time she hit me and I almost had forgotten my place as a daughter. She threw bleach in my face and I had called the police and had her put in jail. My children were tired of having to be embarrassed but I still could not just leave my mother behind with no one. I stayed there for only six months after that, was trying to pursue modeling as well, but this I couldn't do because I had no one to keep my kids. So I had begun looking for local producers to try and network with because I told myself.... I gotta make it somehow, and then I made a decision to move to Columbus, Ohio where I am now. I finally got away from some of the drama but my mother's very ill and I made the choice not to leave her side. I got there and stayed with relatives.

Chapter Twenty Seven

The Withdrawal

MY MOTHER AND I WERE willing to stay in a shelter and asked where some were, but my cousin said that we had to wait a month before we went to a shelter there and we were dumb enough to believe it. Besides the kids didn't want to go to a shelter anyways. My mother soon got really sick and ended up having to be admitted into the hospital. I had gotten a job at a temp service while staying with my cousin. Well my cousin's son had his child's mother staying with him as well and she had one child by him and another little boy by someone else. Her son for some strange reason would hit my baby girl who at the time was just one years old. This was always going on while I would be at work. Of course I was highly upset and I handled this situation completely wrong now that I look back at it but in my mind you should control your son.

I had gotten off of work and came home to find my little girl with a black eye and little white puss coming out of it as if it had gotten infected. I was furious and told her that if she did not keep her son from hitting on my child that I was going to whoop his tail myself! Well she said she would stop this but this little boy just kept on.

So one evening he hit my child again and my middle daughter popped him, when she heard this she became angry but I just didn't care. I was fed up also because while we were staying there some days when I got back from work it was almost as if my kids were ashamed and scared to eat and I know they had food because I had went grocery shopping with my cousin's mom and bought some groceries as well. It was to the point they were saying that this girl was saying mean things to them when I was not around and I literally caught my kids eating in the closet area by the kitchen because they acted as if they were afraid. That's not all. I would get off and my kids would tell me how they were scared to eat anything even though they were fed, I caught my daughter eating in the utility room. This angered me even more.

I was wondering what the heck is really going on while I'm at work? I didn't understand because I may have had it hard as a kid but I treat other's children the way I wanted my own children treated. I was going through too much again. Extremely hot tempered but still keeping my composure.

I was pissed! So I said to her I have been telling you to get your child since I have been here, I will not punish my child when you know your son has the habit of hitting my little girl. Well of coarse this led up to an argument and she just kept getting irate now this woman was eight months pregnant and you're really in my face trying to approach me knowing I'm not going to lift one finger against you...well at least I had some type of sense Jesus gave me. I had enough of jail and would never do that. So I walked away even when she was trying to provoke me to hit her.

But God specifically says in his WORD be slow to speak, slow to wrath and slow to anger so I had to guard my tongue and mind my temper. Meanwhile the devil kept saying just do it. It's obvious that she does not care about her situation. GOD cared and it was he who had to remind me of the children that not only I had but she had of her own.

Well she said get out you and your damn kids and although I had nowhere else and my cousin's mother told me I didn't have to go anywhere I just refused to stay there! Once you say get out to my children and the fact that my kids were being mistreated behind my back anyways I said NO PROBLEM. I went to my middle daughters' school and told them what was going on and they quickly reacted. This man who was a retired officer working there took me to the YWCA and we were taken in. This was humiliating to me and I had no one to really talk to.

I didn't really want anyone to know what was happening. Sky knew about it but was too dealing with alot so he could not help. He felt bad about that. I had to be in the shelter by 5 p.m. and had to be out every morning at 7 a.m. I would drop off the kids at school and my baby girl and I would be at the library while I was job and apartment searching. I always used to pass by this little church when I had to be out and always wanted to attend but I just couldn't bring myself to go inside. I was nervous, and anyways what was I going to do for God?

Me a sinner. Just another lie I allowed the devil to keep telling me and I being spiritually weak didn't know it. I think I stayed there at the shelter for three weeks and had gotten a job at Walmart and an apartment of my own. The girls were so happy to be out of that situation!! But it was me who remained unthankful for what God had done for me. Never satisfied with the blessings he always gave me despite the lessons that I had to learn due to lack of knowledge and understanding. Even as I read the book of proverbs and Ecclesiastes I still had no wisdom and those specific books tell you of the wisdom to be gained as well as what not to do in life.

Chapter Twenty Eight

Throwing In The Towel…

URING THIS TIME I WAS talking to this guy I had met via internet trying to call myself pursuing music. I had given up the modeling idea and just began asking questions about the music industry. He was very well known and I believe he is going to be famous. This man and I had first began communicating when I had first decided to leave and move to Columbus.

So he knew a lot I was going through. Only thing was took me out of my safe zone. See when I first decided to leave I truly stepped out on faith and prayed specifically to GOD and said I was done giving my heart to men who didn't love me and letting them just use my body so I had completely no interest in any man! We had a common interest in music but most of all, we shared a love for GOD!! I had never heard of any young man having a love for GOD as he did at least in my life.

I knew there were some out there but I just never believed I would meet any. Well this man took an interest in me. He said he wanted me and I mean we would be on the phone for hours. Sometimes from 2 in the afternoon until8 in the evening take a break and then he'd call back and we would be on the phone until like 4 in the morning. He talked my head off for three months lol, and we stayed in scripture.

Although I kept telling him no because I didn't trust any man he felt different because of his love for GOD. That's what I needed, or so I thought! He used the same line most guys do....I won't ever hurt you, and trust me I'm different from the rest! The one that really got me was when he said he was a man of GOD! So finally after three months of talking with this man I caved. We had never met and I was head over heels already. Simply because of his love for the LORD.

We always talked about me getting my life together and how I didn't have to feel like nobody cares anymore! And one Sunday morning I got up and felt like I didn't care what anybody else would say about me in the church I needed GOD! So I got the kids ready and we proceeded out of the door got into the car and I went to that church I remembered when I stayed at the shelter. I began to praise GOD more in my life. I had never felt better. But then one night during a phone conversation I began to tell this man how I was ready to meet him and wanted to be with him. He shut me down. I heard another female in the background giving him demands and began questioning who she was and he said the one thing I dreaded ever hearing again. You can never compete with that!

Don't even ask? I said. What did you just say to me? He said I can't be with you. I quickly realized that once he realized that I did not have the finances he'd thought I had and plus with all the problems and issues I had he didn't want me after all. Who was I kidding? I mean you can't really blame anybody for not wanting to be with someone unstable. But my goodness for all this time I felt like you could have been said this to me. After all I told you I had been through you were just the same as all the others.

To me my feeling was we would have been better off by you just understanding when I said I was not ready in the first place instead of leading me on to believe you were really interested. I would have still been his friend just the same and would have fellowshipped with this man in the Lord just the same and I would not have gotten hurt.

But no the ego of some men and most of all myself. Smh. So once again I got angry with God and turned away from his love and everything else. Reason being was because every time I went to pick up my bible to get comfort I was now reminded of him because we had covered a lot of scripture in most I had marked down with a highlighter marker to come back to remember them.

So I had the hurt memories of all the conversations with him. So once again I let that allow me to withdraw from the LORD. I began working at a new job and began sleeping with guys I didn't know again, and drinking to drown out all that had happened. Just the feeling of being held in some ones arms just to feel loved was better than nothing at all to me. My self- esteem was completely shot.

I was wrapped back up into a world of fornication, perversion, and sin. Drinking and not caring about myself. I said as long as I go to work and raise my kids I was cool. See one thing I can truly say is my kids never saw me laid up with these random men but what I was doing was still no excuse just because I didn't ever bring any home. Still Sodom and Gomorrah bound.

One night I went to my cousin's and kicked it with the younger group of young males cousin's and two of their friends.

Chapter Twenty Nine

My Dignity....

I WAS ALREADY DRUNK WHEN I got there. Well I ended up drinking more and by the time I knew it my little cousin asked me if he could make a run in my car and I said yes. But not trusting him fully because he had no license nor the other three I decided to roll with them. He went where he needed to go and then we went over to his sister's house.

Once we got inside we were still drinking and I wanting to hear music and loving to dance began dancing to some Latino music. Well one of his friends got up from the couch and began dancing with me so I was picking at him saying how he can't dance. At that moment his other friend got up and said I got this.

They were all around their twenties I had no business even being there but I figured I was with my little cousins so it was cool.

The dance was over and I proceeded out the door but was staggering, that's when the eldest out of the two of my little cousins said cuz I'm not letting you drive like that! I told him well I at least needed to lay down to sleep it off and he said just go lay down in the back. So I did just that it wasn't ten minutes that I passed out drunk.

I kept feeling someone touching me as I slept. And I was moaning and mumbling. I remember being kissed and someone feeling on my breasts but I was too darn drunk to wake up completely. I felt my pants and panties coming down and they were at this point off. I woke up completely and it was this young man I had danced with. I had the strength of a drunkard trying to push this young man off me but it was like I was a little rickety rag doll.

I he was holding my hands and saying you know you want it and I could not get him off me. It just happened. I just went on and let him after that. And when I looked up I saw my two little cousins standing there in the door watching and laughing.

I was humiliated, devastated and embarrassed. Most of all my dignity was gone. He didn't even have the decency to use a condom. I laid there when it was over for a minute in shock that I had gotten drunk and allowed myself in this position and by my own little cousin's friend while they watched the entire thing! I sat up, put on my clothes, came out of the room and just stared at them and asked why did you do this?

No one said a word, I could see the guilt in their faces. After that I had no words and just slammed the door as hard as I could, got in the car and drove myself home in tears. I felt just as guilty as they were because I didn't have to put myself in that predicament in the first place....but I was just in disbelief that my own little cousins were just like the older male relatives in our family and it was a family trait! The chain was not officially broken.

I got home showered and when my male friend called me he could tell something was wrong with me. I tried was trying to hide it but he had this way of making me spill the beans. I told him and he was furious! Boy I didn't hear the end of it.

What he didn't know was how I felt inside. Disgust, mocked yet again, and disrespected as well as ashamed! You would have thought I had learned my lesson but no this did not stop my rebellion.

I ended up late from my period and thought this young man had knocked me up. I felt total guilt so I called a rape hotline and described everything that had happened. I felt like it was my fault but she reminded me that no matter rather I was drunk and hanging out with the younger crowd or not this young man violated me and those that watched it happen were just as wrong! I told her I felt responsible and that's why I didn't call the police.

She said most women feel that way but that I should've still called. I explained that I feared I may have been pregnant and I never had an abortion but if so I didn't want it. What was I to do? She to my surprise was a Christian so of course the response was that abortion was out of the question. And although I was not a faithful Christian I had to agree with her.

So I considered adoption. But once she and I got off the phone I thought of me as a child and what it was like for me in foster care so I just threw that option out of the window.

At that moment I realized it was me and Jesus. He was all I had! So I prayed hard with all I had and asked the Lord to spare me a child of rape for I couldn't bare it. GOD heard me and it turned out I was not pregnant!!! I had never thanked him so much! But did this stop me from still searching? No it didn't. It had been a year and I was still talking to this man on the phone.

Chapter Thirty

The Shame and Cry For Help...

WE BEGAN TO ARGUE SO much it was almost routine. Eventually we began disrespecting one another and calling one another out of our names. He would try to tell me about changing and GOD and in the same breath put me down! Then he would apologize then I would say hurtful things to try and hurt him because I was hurt by how he didn't want me and lied to me. I had become pushy and irate.

I began seeing this young man at my place of employment. In my mind all men were dogs. I just wanted him for one thing. Funny thing though. My ego as a woman would not prove me from wanting to have him even and I didn't even want him? Vanity.

The lust I had grew and I became jealous of the situation I myself had created because of hatred and rage again. So for the first time in my life I told this man I was pregnant. I thought I really was but even after I had gotten my monthly situation even though I was a week late, I still lied but only because I did not want anyone else to have him.

My mind kept saying, I want him to be miserable. All men should be miserable because of the pain they inflict on the lives of their children's mother's and the lies they tell. Now you tell me who was really doing the thinking for me at that time?

Then the phone calls stopped and I was back doing my thing. Only difference was I was back to trying to model and still fornicating. Till one day I got tired. I just went back to church and sat there listening and crying because after everything I still needed GOD!! He was always there even when I disobeyed him and had chosen not to listen. I began thinking about all of the times I was homeless, hungry, ashamed, talked about, turned away, beat up, raped, broken and bruised. Eventually we became friends again and we remain friends to this day. I was able to let it go but now I know I am growing closer to GOD and just grow and allow him to heal me completely. Walked away from old habits and am a receptionist. Encouraging the next young mother in JESUS and praying for them too. Asking for prayer for us all including me and just getting closer in finding out more of GOD'S love.

Actually GOD had to remind me of soo many times I often left my first love and still he would always come to get me. I was being and behaving at the time as a harlot throughout most of my life. Cheating on GOD with my mind, heart, and body. Giving myself over to the things of this world that can never guarantee me a seat in heaven. Just like in the book of Hosea. Laying in my own filth of lust a whoredom, desperation to have someone love me, not realizing GOD had formed me in the womb and watched me grow into the lost individual just waiting on me to heed his words and seek out his love. I often wondered why things had never worked out with any of these men? Well....I was not used to obedience. I was NOT listening to GOD at all.

Chapter Thirty One

The Healing Process....

I SAID TO GOD IN my heart... all this time I was running from you and running to these people who could have cared less rather I existed or not, and here it was your door that was always open. Where was my mind all this time? Was I that blind that I could not see you really loved me? I felt like the prodigal son. Who when he had gotten his inheritance, he had went off on his own and when he returned from being foolish with nothing, his Father when seeing him ran to him in joy for his return! Still embracing him with loving arms no matter what he did! Fed him, clothed him, and just was happy to see his child home and alive! That's when I realized that is the same love GOD had for me and so much more! I belonged to him and didn't have to run into anyone else arms but his.

My situations in life could have been so much worse and that there are other brothers and sisters in this world facing so much more! And here it was I was giving up on my life. Some women and children murdered and raped, beaten to death, shot and much more but it was GOD who kept his hands on me!

GOD is just as alive today as he is in yesterday! All I had to do was give my life unto the LORD JESUS CHRIST and stop running. And I have been content with that ever since. Because now there is meaning. GOD told me that my body ids my temple and I should not defile it. When you sin against your temple which is in the body, you sin against GOD because his spirit is within you. That's why when GOD says this to us it is so very IMPORTANT!

Is money, fame, fortune, greed, lust, fornication, adultery, rape, murder, violence, and just having someone to lay up with worth an eternity in the KINGDOM OF HEAVEN WITH YAHWEH? No it's not, at least not to me! Because GOD does not lie. From dust we were made and to dust we shall return! No worldly thing is worth GOD not hearing your cry! Or going to Hell! I had enough pain and hurt here on earth and that was never GOD'S intent for you or me.

He does not want us to suffer but sometimes he allows these things to strengthen us and sometimes he lets us get just what we ask for when we are not obedient. For our parents choices we are not responsible but for our own we do have a choice.

See I realize that for years I used to blame my mother for everything but I didn't realize that she did not have anyone. Yes she could have chosen better in life but sometimes when you are searching and don't know what you're searching for you become more and more lost to even yourself. GOD to me is the only husband, father, and true friend I have ever known. Everyone one else has turned their backs on me but JESUS is the only love

I have ever known who remains always. TURN BACK THY HEART UNTO OUR LORD AND LET HIM LOVE AND SAVE YOU!

And this world can be wicked. I now realize that only JESUS is perfect and this perfect man and perfect love I've been searching for can only be found in him and though I am still discovering him and all his majesty and glory I know it was he who kept me and I gotta lot of recovering, healing, forgiving, loving, and changing to do so I am starting my new journey. Some days I get these memories and they still hurt. The blessing is that I finally found a wonderful church home and family. But it's not about the church because even churches and the people in them run folks back to the streets by judging them and condemning them.

Or it's who wears the best clothing…No I tell you it is GOD'S words and the spiritual food to the soul you get in the church… It's GOD'S WORDS which explains to us the importance of our faith and the Glory of the LORD thy true and living GOD! I was so lost and still at times have trouble trusting people and even letting someone love me.

Chapter Thirty Two

Forgiveness and
a New Beiginning!

B UT GOD ALLOWED ME TO see that He loves me, my children love me, my mom, the only sister and best friend Fiona Marie I still have that didn't abandon me.

I could never ask for a better place to be than with GOD and all his majesty and all his glory! By believing in him and keeping all his laws and being obedient to his will you will have a better life. And even more he is the living water to drink from GOD'S cup is to have everlasting life! Worship him and you will see. Try it instead of putting all of your time into worldly things. JESUS said in JOHN CHAPTER 4 VERSES 13-14 WHOSOEVER DRINKETH OF THE WATER THAT I SHALL GIVE HIM SHALL NEVER THIRST: BUT THE WATER THAT I SHALL GIVE HIM SHALL BE IN HIM A WELL OF WATER SPRINGING UP INTO EVERLASTING LIFE.

The destroyer wants you to keep listening to the music to keep you dumbfounded and reading the junk in the tabloids or the reality television shows, and latest fashions.

And if you don't feel comfortable at church at first like I did, start by reading your bible and getting saved! Praying to the LORD, talking to him like you would anyone else in a regular conversation!

He is always available and his door is always open all you have to do is talk to him and believe! And trust me there's power in prayer! Repent and confess thy sins. I still do this when I mess up and get in my flesh. People often make the mistake of thinking we Christians are perfect, well were not! If that were true GOD would not have had to send his only son so that we could make it back into the Kingdom of heaven. For he knew we were full of sin and could not enter without it.

That is why GOD'S WORD always refers to us being washed by the blood of the Lamb which is the blood of JESUS. And when we mess up GOD allows us to come repent unto him and he polishes us right back up and says, NOW LET'S TRY IT AGAIN!

And no that does not mean that he does not expect change because he does! But our GOD is so merciful he gives us the chance of making a change every day when we wake up to see another day when he breathes into our bodies. We have to truly count it all joy and count our blessings! He does not want any of his children to spend their eternity in a burning hell. The greatest gift is to choose life and to choose life is to choose JESUS!

It's not about money because you were born in this world naked and naked you shall return so what is the point. You are supposed to make a life for yourself and especially work hard at pursuing your goals, but many people make the mistake of letting money consume them. You must always remember GOD first before anything! GOD can give wealth and blessings too!

But remember to put him first above all Thou shalt love the Lord thy GOD with all thy heart and all thy soul and only him shall thy serve! Don't abuse your blessings and especially one another! Love thy neighbor as thyself, treat others with, loving kindness, forgive and be forgiven, honor thy mother and thy father....boy did I really need to learn that one Thank You Jesus, pray for those that spitefully use you and persecute you for many will hate you and shame you for the righteousness of Christ is within you and because you follow Christ you will be hated and in a lot of cases judged. But remember this no one can judge you but CHRIST and you gotta keep pressing for the LORD! You can do it. GOD'S Love is Freedom! Eternal life GOD offers he loves you and I just that much. Lord knows I'm still a work in progress but if GOD can save me he can surely save his other billions of children including you! I had to learn to stop the hatred towards others and the violence.

And learning what love truly is. Love is my daughters running to my arms when they are happy, sad, or bruised. Love is forgiving those that may have caused you so much pain or the pain you inflicted on others. Love is giving strength and encouragement to other's when the rest of the world closes the door on them and won't feed or clothe them. Love is compassion and guidance. Love does not hurt you and love well...Love is JESUS! GOD cries because he LOVES US SO MUCH AND GIVES US THIS LOVE NO MATTER WHAT WE DO BUT SO MANY OF HIS CHILDREN ARE TURNING THEIR BACKS ON HIM. NOT READING HIS WORD OR WORSHIPPING THE ONLY TRUE GOD WHO BREATHES LIFE INTO ALL PEOPLE EVERYDAY EVEN THE WICKED HE STILL

LOVES AND PEOPLE CHOSE NOT TO LISTEN TO HIS WORDS. SOME PEOPLE WOULD RATHER CHOSE TO LIVE A LIFE OF UNRIGHTEOUSNESS RATHER THAN THE LIVING WORD OF JESUS? BUT EVEN STILL HE LOVES YOU. AFTER EVERYTHING HE ENDURED FOR US AND PEOPLE STILL WOULD RATHER TURN AWAY TO EVIL. PEOPLE BETTER WAKE UP BECAUSE WE ARE DEFINITELY FACING TIMES OF PROPHECY RIGHT NOW, RIGHT NOW!! READ THE BOOK OF REVELATIONS AND ESPECIALLY CHAPTER 13. GOD IS GIVING US THE ONLY CHANCE BY CHOSING TO BE SAVED THROUGH JESUS CHRIST!

I'm not done on my journey and I still left some of the things I used to do out. I was not a saint and still am no saint. But I've told you as much as I could. So where am I now? Well my sisters and brothers, I am still pressing on and I am singing my praises to our Father GOD in heaven his majesty! I may have not become a Marine Biologist, but I am a proud mother of three beautiful daughters!

With the help of GOD himself and me being a willing vessel in testimony I offer to let young girls know that it's plenty of us out here who searched for love in all the wrong places but if you just give God your heart you will find real love and you don't have to sell yourself to get it, IT'S FREE! I am a first time writer and just wanted to tell my story. I am singing my praises to JESUS and thanking him even for the storm because I've realized that he is the only father, friend, lawyer, lover, healer, doctor, and judge I have truly ever had! I regret not one thing not even the struggles because GOD got my full attention and it was my lesson to learn.

I am not a perfect Christian but am indeed a Christian and a child of the one true GOD in all his glory and there's work to be done. I wanna tell you all that I love you and we all get angry at each other and a lot of times about our childhoods or many other reasons. Some of you may grow weary as I did and your heart may even begin to harden.

But I just want to encourage you and tell you never give up!! Keep on praying and praising Jesus even in the midst of the storm, because Jesus is the only one who can calm the storm! Young women and especially single mother's and anyone who's been through child abuse, it's very wrong what has happened this is true but what's in the dark will always be brought forth into the light. Don't be afraid to cry because crying is healing.

Don't be afraid to talk to someone because you may be too afraid of what they may say or if they will believe you! And don't be afraid to forgive them for they know not what they do and even more so don't be afraid to fight back! You may be afraid because you may think that you are fighting alone, but you are not. CHRIST JESUS is with you all you have to do is go to him and believe.

Prayer....

(Free Will) To Have The Living Water & True Life!

Ask the LORD to come into your life and tell JESUS you believe in him and that you believe he shed his blood on the cross for you.

That you want him as a part of your life every day for as long as you live! Most people think that because of their sins they can't come to GOD but that's just another guilt trip lie they adversary Satan would like for you to keep believing. So if you really want to change and want to know and except JESUS as your LORD AND SAVIOR, please recite this prayer.

YOU ARE THE CHRIST THE SON OF THE LIVING GOD (MATTHEW 16:16) FATHER GOD! THANK YOU GOD FOR YOUR GRACE OF SALVATION.

YOU HAVE FORGIVEN MY SINS. I THANK YOU THAT YOU HAVE MADEME A CHILD OF GOD AND THAT YOU HAVE COMPLETELY FREED ME FROM ALL SUFFERING,

CURSES AND THE AUTHORITY OF SATAN (JOHN 1:12, ROMANS 8:15)

JESUS YOU ARE LIVING IN ME THROUGH YOUR HOLY SPIRIT AND YOU WILL BE WITH ME FOREVER, JESUS YOU ARE THE SON OF GOD WHO WORKSAND GUIDES ME JOHN 14:16-17)

WHEN I PRAY IN THE NAME OF JESUS CHRIST YOU ANSWER MY PRAYERS (JOHN 14:14, 15:17, REVELATION 8:3-5)

ALL THE FORCES OF SATAN, THE DEVIL, AND DEMONS ARE BOUND AND ARE COMPLETELY DRIVEN OUT WHEN I PRAY IN THE NAME OF JESUS CHRIST (1JOHN 3:8, PSALMS 103:20-22)

I THANK YOU THAT YOU HAVE GIVEN ME THE CITIZENSHIP OF HEAVEN (PHILLIPIANS 3:20)

I THANK YOU THAT YOU HAVE CALLED ME AS A WITNESS OF THIS GOSPEL AND AS A MAIN CHARACTER FOR YOUR EVANGELIZATION. (MATTHEW 28:16-20)

EVERYWHERE I GO PLEASE SEND YOUR HOLY ANGELS CHARGE OVER ME AND MY LIFE TO PROTECT, SHEILD, AND BREAKDOWN ALL THE FORCES OF DARKNESS, THE DEVIL AND THE DEMONS IN THE NAME OF JESUS CHRIST AND LET ME BE FILLED WITH THE HOLY SPIRIT OF JESUS CHRIST. LET ALL MY DISBELIEF AND ALL THE FORCES OF CURSES IN MY FAMILY AND FAMILY LINE BE COMPLETELY BROKEN IN THE NAME OF JESUS CHRIST. I PRAY IN THE NAME OF JESUS CHRIST MY LORD AND SAVIOR AMEN.

If you believe the lies the devil keeps trying to feed your mind and do not allow JESUS in your heart you will be giving the devil just what he wants, to keep you away from confessing your sins and going to GOD! Don't believe the lies and most of all be righteous and don't doubt GOD and say well I am not perfect and can't talk to anyone about JESUS because my life's not all the way right. Guess what? NO ONE but JESUS IS perfect! So don't let anyone tell you he won't hear you…NONE OF US ARE PERFECT!! YOU KEEP ON PRESSING and CALL ON THE LORD THY GOD, I cannot stress that enough!!! I still get angry and upset too we all do but the key is to humble ourselves and remember GOD'S LOVE, MERCY, and FOLLOW GOD's PATH of RIGHTEOUSNESS AS MUCH AS YOU CAN!! He knows were not perfect, again that's the reason JESUS had to come on our behalf and inteerceed to be the sacrifice and his blood was shed for OUR SINS! Love one another more and stop the hatred. YAHWEH LOVES YOU, brothers and sisters!!

Mom I forgive you and I apologize for all the hurt I've ever caused and not understanding until I myself had to go down my own path. Dad I forgive you and may you rest in peace. I love you both!

To my siblings I love you. To my kids father's GOD is STRONG and UNFAILING! To my daughters…You are the love I was searching for and never knew it! GOD did hear me and each time though my life was hard he gave me life. And his love he put inside of you and in your eyes his love was there this entire time and I could not realize what it was GOD was saying…TRUST IN ME my child. STOP RUNNING! SEEK ME AND YOU WILL FIND ME BUT SEEK WORLDY THINGS AND YOU WILL SURELY FIND THEM! ALWAYS LISTEN TO GOD… SEEK HIM AND HIS LOVE ONLY because in the end HIS LOVE IS EVERLASTING!

And to the only father I have ever known. THANK YOU JESUS FOR ALWAYS BEING PATIENT WITH ME and NEVER LEAVING ME ...FOR I LEFT YOU MANY TIMES BUT YOU HAVE NEVER LEFT ME! I REPENT MY SINS AND CONFESS MY UNPERFECT LOVE TO YOU IN FRONT OF THE ENTIRE WORLD MY KING AND GLORY BE TO YOU GOD IN HEAVEN! I HONOR YOU AND YOUR HOLY SPIRIT OF YAHWEH FOR CHANGING MY HEART, MIND, AND SPIRIT!

Your daughter always ELISHEVA! I never really knew peace until I found you. I used to pray but didn't believe. You sent your words and sought after me through people some of whom I would just meet and would just say kind words like the LORD is with you! I thought it had to be a burning bush that you would bring to speak to me but it was the vessels of people sent forth by the LORD THY GOD and often times we don't even realize it.

But I must say it's important for us all to read your Words my LORD because many will come in your name and are not of you LORD GOD. You saw me that day by the ocean waters and as the waves flowed back and forth over my feet I felt your nostrils breathing on me as the wind blew. I felt closer to you as I watched the sun set and saw how beautiful thou truly are!! You the Father and creator of all life and things!

As I strolled down the beach I remembered the poem footprints when the person walking only notices one set of footprints and LORD it was you who reminded him that the reason there was that one set of footprints was because you were carrying him the whole time. I knew you were there and so you still are my LORD! I know you LIVE!!

You love your people and they will see that you LIVE! You GOD are merciful and forgiver of all sins. You make all things new! You made me new!! You accept me and love me the way I am and it's going to be alright. Stop looking to man and come into the arms of our loving Father and so I have been seeking after you LORD. BLESSED IS THE NAME OF THE LORD THY GOD WHO LIVES FOREVER!! Amen!

(My Father Loves Me) No mortal man can ever Love or understand me the way you do JESUS!!!

Woman who art fragile...LIFT THYSELF UP! Why do you mourn in your heart for the men of this world? For the troubles that you have faced **dont** you know that it is I that breathe life into you so that you will profess my words for I alone have not nor will ever forsake you! Some people know not how to handle this type of heart for it is peculiar and a rarity.

Wipe thy eyes for have made you my bride and are chosen in a new creation of my son CHRIST JESUS washed by the Blood of the LAMB, I will heal thee you are clean!

CPSIA information can be obtained at www.ICGtesting.com
Printed in the USA
BVOW03s0701110215

387005BV00013B/4/P

9 781458 210203